KII

Fo

TA

Best Wishes

Sally.

2014

KILDARE
FOLK
TALES

STEVE LALLY

The
History
Press
Ireland

This book is dedicated to my beautiful little girl, Isabella Grace.
'For you I would fight the Devil himself.'

To my mother, Nuala Lally, who felt the same sorrow
that broke the heart of Queen Buan.

This book is also dedicated to the memory of my great friend
Peter O'Toole, who passed away long before his time in 1994.
'Wish you were here …'

First published 2014

The History Press Ireland
50 City Quay
Dublin 2
Ireland
www.thehistorypress.ie

© Steve Lally, 2014
Illustrations © Steve Lally, 2014

The right of Steve Lally to be identified as the Author
of this work has been asserted in accordance with the
Copyright, Designs and Patents Act 1988.

British Library Cataloguing in Publication Data.
A catalogue record for this book is available from the British Library.

ISBN 978 1 84588 810 7

Typesetting and origination by The History Press

CONTENTS

ACKNOWLEDGEMENTS

I would like to thank the following people for helping me along this journey:

Criostoir Mac Cartaigh, Archive-Collector, National Folklore Collection at UCD; Jack Lynch, master storyteller, for his help and encouragement; Seamus Cullen, local historian and a legend in his own time; Mario Corrigan, wise man of Kildare and executive librarian at Kildare County Council, for his patience and guidance; Liz Weir, master storyteller, for always lighting the way; Nandi Jola, storyteller, poet and muse; James Durney, author and historian; The County Kildare Archaeological Society; all the staff at Banbridge Library County Down; Chad Buterbaugh, folklorist and friend; my Aunt Eileen, who always brings light into the darkness; and all my friends and family for their support, and all those people who listen to my stories and give them life, for without you it would all be ashes in the wind.

INTRODUCTION

As a storyteller, it has always been my passion to hear new tales and find out more about strange and wondrous characters that exist or existed in the world around me. Stories are vitally important in keeping the spirit and charm of a place alive and to get the opportunity to collect and write stories from County Kildare has been a real gift. Growing up there, in a small townland called Rathcoffey, the country and its folklore still resonates within my very soul.

Writing this book has created a unique opportunity to get in touch with the county and the people that I grew up with in a way that transcends all conventional conviviality, for there were chances to meet people and visit places that existed hundreds even thousands of years ago and I feel honoured to be able to tell their tales.

There was chance to cheer on Dan Donnelly, the King of the Curragh; witness the charms of Moll Anthony; ride upon the back of the Pooka Horse; and shake hands with the Wizard Earl of Kildare. I even came face to face with 'Auld Nick, The Black Earl of Hell'. All of these characters are immortalised in illustrations that hide between the pages, waiting to be revealed.

There were opportunities to return to all the places I played in as a child and revisit the magic that is childhood. Possibilities to visit loved ones who have passed on, listen to all the old songs and poems again and read the wonderful stories written by children almost eighty years ago.

On this fantastic journey I met with some great people too, including folklorists, storytellers, archaeologists, scholars, historians and just some truly fascinating and amazing characters.

It is said that Kildare is the most haunted county in Ireland and this may well be so with the Death Coach trundling through the long acre, the white lady roaming the lonely country roads and the ghosts who haunt Clongowes and Maynooth College. Kildare also has some of the finest wonder tales in the world.

It has been a great experience and an emotional one too; to be reminded of times of great joy and great sadness. They are part of the same story and it is because of the story that I returned here in the first place.

A big thank you to everyone who helped me along the way, and may the road rise with you …

Steve Lally, 2014

1

Dan Donnelly, the King of the Curragh

I wish to dedicate this story to Seamus McCormick, Owen Murphy and the Sacred Heart Boxing Club, Newry. For they taught me to stand tall and face my fears with courage and dignity.

The Ballad of Dan Donnelly

Come all you true-born Irishmen wherever ye be,
I pray you give attention; and listen unto me;
It's of as true a story as ever you did hear,
About Donnelly and Cooper that fought at Kildare.
'Twas on the third of June, my boys the challenge was sent o'er,
From Britannia to old Granua to raise her sons once more,
To renew their satisfaction, and their credit to recall;
So they were in distraction since bold Donnelly conquered all.
When Granua read the challenge, and received it with a smile,
You had better haste into Kildare, my well-beloved child,
It's there you will reign victorious, as you have always done before,
And your deeds will shine most glorious all around Hibernia's shore.
The challenge was accepted, and those noble lads did prepare,

To meet with Captain Kelly on the Curragh of Kildare.

The Englishmen bet ten to one that day against poor Dan,

But such odds as these would never dismay the blood of Irishman.

When these two bully champions they stripped in the ring,

They faced each other manfully, and to work they did begin,

From six till nine they sparred on, till Danny knocked him down,

Well done, my child, Granua smiled, this is ten thousand pounds.

The second round that Cooper fought he knocked down Donnelly,

But Dan had steel likewise true game, and rose most manfully,

Right active then was Cooper and knocked Donnelly down once more

The English they all cried out, the battle you may give o'er.

The cheering of those English peers did make the valleys sound,

While their English champion kept prancing on the ground.

Full ten to one they freely bet, on the ground whereon they stand,

That their brave hero would soon deceive their boasting Irishman.

Long life to Miss Kelly, she recorded on the plain,

She boldly stepped into the ring, saying, Dan, what do you mean?

Saying, Dan, my boy, what do you mean, Hibernia's son, says she,

My whole estate I've bet on you, brave Donnelly.

When Donnelly received the fall after the second round,

He spoke to Captain Kelly, as he lay on the ground,

Saying, do not fear, for I'm not beat, although I got two falls,

I'll let them know, before I go, I'll make them pay for all.

I'm not afraid, brave Donnelly, Miss Kelly she did say,

For I have bet my coach and four that you may gain the day;

You are a true born Irishman, the gentry well do know,

And on the plains of sweet Kildare this day their valour show.

Donnelly rose up again, and meeting with great might,

For to surprise the nobles all he continued for to fight,

Cooper stood on his own defence, exertion proved in vain,

He then received a temple blow that reeled him on the plain.

Ye sons of proud Britannia, your boasting now give o'er,

Since by our hero Donnelly, your hero is no more;

In eleven rounds he got nine knocks down, besides broke his jawbone
Shake hands, says she, brave Donnelly, the battle is our own.

Anonymous

Growing up in Kildare I had heard enigmatic tales about the great boxer Dan Donnelly from the old-timers. I was always fascinated and when I heard that his arm was kept somewhere in the Curragh, this drove my curiosity even further. People talked about him like one would speak of a fictional superhero or a brave character from some film epic.

Who was this Dan Donnelly and why was and is he so revered both in Kildare and boxing folklore? Like Mohammed Ali, 'Sir Dan' was not only a champion of sport but a champion of the people. This is his story.

Dan Donnelly (March 1788–18 February 1820) was a pioneering pugilist and was Ireland's first home-grown boxing heavyweight champion. In 2008 Donnelly's name was entered into the 'International Boxing Hall of Fame' under the category of 'Boxing Pioneers'.

He was born into a poor Dublin family who lived in the city's violent and deprived docklands. His father was a carpenter and found it very hard to make ends meet due to the fact he had seventeen children and suffered from very poor health. It is speculated that he suffered from bronchitis, so the breathing in of sawdust combined with the extreme physical labour meant that he was often incapable of holding down the job.

With little or no income, the Donnelly family were always just one step away from the workhouse. Poverty pervaded Dublin at the end of the eighteenth century and Dan, like may other children of his day, went to work in his father's trade as soon as he was old enough.

Little did Dan know that the shadow of political revolution would come looking for him. In 1803, a group of Irish nationalists, including Robert Emmet, Thomas Russell and James Hope, made an attempt to secure Ireland's independence from the United Kingdom. The revolt failed and, despite going into hiding, Emmet was captured, tried and executed in Dublin by hanging and beheading for the crime of high treason on 20 September 1803.

Donnelly, like Mohammed Ali, realised he lived in a country that had no one to represent its people and that they were regarded as second-class citizens. The country was in desperate need for someone to come along and give the British a black eye. Dan was very proud of Ireland and its people; he wanted to give the Irish a sense of pride and self-respect at a time when it was badly needed. He hated nothing more than unfairness and to see advantage being taken of the weak and vulnerable. He was a proud man with high morals and principles and no lion could display more fury than Dan Donnelly when he witnessed what he considered to be blatant bullying.

Dan was not an easy man to get a rise out of and he would do whatever it took to bring peace and harmony to an otherwise potentially violent situation. On the rough Dublin streets he was constantly goaded to fight due to his great athletic stature, but when pushed too far he would make short work of his tormentors. After a while Dan got a name as a fine street fighter and defender of those weaker and more vulnerable than most. In fact, he became a bit of a celebrity amongst the people in his locality.

On one occasion, upon hearing the screams of a young woman down at the dockside area where he lived, Dan went to investigate and found two sailors attacking a girl. He witnessed them throw the poor girl into the River Liffey, so he dived in after her and pulled her out, saving her life.

Unluckily for the exhausted Dan the thugs were waiting for him when he climbed out. They grabbed him, attacked him with stones and kicked him. His arm was so badly damaged that one would have thought it impossible that he should become Ireland's greatest boxer of his time. Fortunately for Dan, he was found by some good people and taken to Dr Steeven's Hospital (which still stands to this day beside St James' Gate, where Guinness is produced and opposite Heuston railway station). He was treated by the renowned surgeon Dr Abraham Colles, best known for his 'Treatise on Surgical Anatomy' (1811).

Colles was well known for his compassion towards the city's poor and when he heard about the great act of selfless courage that the young Donnelly had performed he promised to do what he could to save the arm.

On first seeing the injury Dr Colles was sure that he would have to amputate it; but he decided to try to save the limb and with artistic precision and delicate dexterity he mended Donnelly's arm. When he was done, he affectionately put his arm around Dan and said he was nothing short of a 'Pocket Hercules'. Dan Donnelly was to be another one of Dublin's poor to thank the great Kilkenny-born doctor for his skill and kindness. I am sure Donnelly would have been knocked out again if he knew the magnitude of the man who had saved his arm. For Abraham Colles came from a long line of surgeons and he was twice president of the Royal College of Surgeons in Dublin. Widely acclaimed as a medical researcher and graphic lecturer, one of his papers on the fracture of a forearm bone was so highly acclaimed that the term *Colles Fracture* is still used to this day all over the world. But then one could argue that Colles would have passed out himself if he knew he had saved the arm of the future heavyweight boxing champion and legend of the sport.

Dan was to become the people's champion and a hero to those who could not fight for themselves. There are many stories in regard to this fact and one that stands out involves an old neighbour of his in Dublin, who had died in terrible impoverished conditions.

This neighbour was an elderly lady who lived on Townsend Street and, like sweet Molly Malone, she died of a fever and no one could save her. Because everybody was so terrified of being infected by the contagious disease, not a single soul would come forward to claim or remove the body of the deceased. When the bold Dan heard about this he was disgusted at the inhumanity of it all, especially knowing that the old woman in question was a kind and giving soul who would have gone out of her way to help any of her neighbours. So he took it upon himself to go to the woman's house and lift the remains. He wrapped her body in a blanket and put her over one of his broad shoulders. With that, he proceeded to take her corpse to a local churchyard. When he got there, he found some gravediggers in the process of digging a fresh grave. Dan announced that wished to put the woman's body into the new grave. The gravediggers were not at all pleased with this and dismissed him as a madman.

He looked at them firmly and told them if they did not step aside, they would be occupying the grave and went on to say that this was a land of equality and that this woman had as much right to buried in this grave as anyone. The grave-diggers stood back as Donnelly grabbed a shovel from one of them and proceeded to bury the woman.

Donnelly was nearly six feet tall, and with a powerful, physical build. He weighed almost fourteen stone and had the heart of a lion. Fearless, strong and brave, Dan knew he had the makings of a great fighter. Ironically he was not comfortable with this, as it went against his principles and his disregard for violence. His strongest trait was his outgoing, friendly and sociable personality, and his strong sense of right and wrong. He had many friends and was very popular with all those who knew him. But, human nature being what it is, others around him saw this as a threat and a challenge and felt he should be taken down a peg or two.

There was an incident that took place when Dan was in his early twenties, while having a drink with his sick father, Joseph Donnelly, by the docks. Joseph took a fit of coughing. A brutish sailor who had just come off a boat saw this and began to mimic and berate the poor man. Dan begged the sailor to show some respect and leave his father be. According to the writer Patrick Myler in his book *Dan Donnelly 1788-1820 Pugilist, Publican, Playboy* the sailor replied by saying, 'Any cheek from you, me young bucko, and I'll teach you a lesson in respect'. Dan replied, 'I have no desire to fight you, but if it's what you want, then I'll not back down'. The sailor ran at Donnelly with a terrible roar, but Dan did not budge. He met the madman with a powerful right-hand punch. He broke the sailor's nose but, with blood streaming down his face, the sailor got to his feet and came at young Dan again. A terrible fight took place, lasting for over fifteen minutes, until the sailor could take no more and muttered the word 'enough' through bloody, swollen lips.

It was not long before word got out about Dan and how he dealt with the bully. The violent gangs and hard men of Dublin were intrigued by this new scrapper in town. They were also interested to hear that he was doing what the local constabulary could not do in regard to keeping the streets safe from their kind.

There was one particular character who was considered to be the best boxer in the city and had yet to be beaten.

He was not to happy with all the great praise that Dan was getting. It seemed that in every bar and tavern he frequented he heard tall tales about Donnelly's exploits. So he decided that he would have to put him in his place. He toured through the city streets and went to all the haunts where he knew Dan frequented, announcing that he was demanding to face Dan in a fight. When Dan got word of this he declined, as he did not see himself as a man who would fight for the entertainment and sport of others. When the other man heard of Dan's reply he scoffed and deemed him a yellow-bellied coward with no guts. This was said in front of Dan's family and friends. Dan was furious and agreed to fight the man in order to save his honour. It was then announced that a fight would take place along the banks of the Grand Canal in Dublin. The people of the city were full of great excitement at the news of this epic event.

When the two combatants met by the canal, Dan tried his best to talk his opponent out of this foolish display of aggression. However, the other was not interested in such cowardly talk and threw the first punch. At first Dan did not engage, dancing around the ring, avoiding punches and throwing none himself. This caused the audience to become frustrated and hurl abuse at him. What the audience did not realise was that this was a brilliant tactic, as Donnelly was tiring out his opponent and he made a fast, powerful attack in the sixteenth round. He knocked his opponent to the ground, after which he was unable to get to his feet. Donnelly was declared the new Champion of the City. After that there were no more challenges and Donnelly was more than happy with this.

Meanwhile in an English tavern a wealthy Irish nobleman called Captain William Kelly, overheard English pugilists talking with affiliates of what was known as 'The Fancy' (affluent dandies who supported and sponsored boxing during the eighteenth and nineteenth centuries). Kelly was horrified to hear them poking fun at Mother Ireland and her brave children, stating there was not a courageous man amongst them. They also said that they had gone to Ireland and issued open challenges to the best pugilists there, but no one accepted. What would one expect from a nation of conquered cowards?

Furious at the slander of his native land, Kelly was determined to find a fighting Irishman to take up the challenge. His search eventually took him to Dublin and to Dan Donnelly. Kelly went with his friend Robert Barclay Allardice, a Scotsman, who had heard of this fine young fighter. Allardice was better known as Captain Barclay. He was a renowned long-distance walker and trained many great pugilists. They were told that their man would not come easy as he was very much against the idea of fighting. When they arrived in Dublin they did not have much trouble finding their quarry at the carpenter's yard. But as expected, Dan Donnelly was not interested in fighting. He apologised to the two men for wasting their time and explained that he was a man of peace. But Kelly did not wish to return to England without a fighter who would prove those English dandies wrong. He tried to win Donnelly over by telling him how he would follow in the footsteps of Ireland's great warriors and mythical heroes such as Cuchulainn and Finn McCool. He told him of the epic battles and conquests that ancient Ireland was so famous for and now through Dan they could bring back this sense of pride and deference that had been lost by the Irish people after so many years of oppression. Kelly told Dan that he would bring fire back into the bellies of the Irish people and there was also a fair few bob to be made out it too. Dan was silent and then told Kelly he would think about it for a while.

He came back with: 'Gentlemen, I shall first return to you my sincere thanks for the great dependence you have on my country. The honour you have bestowed on me shall ever be cherished in my bosom. To appear before a multitude of spectators on a plain is wholly against my will, yet my country claims my support.' Dan then clenched his fists and raised his right arm, quivering with the passion of a man about to go into battle and he made this oath: 'I owe no spleen to Great Britain, but the man of any nation who presumes to offer insult to my country, this arm, while my life blood flows, shall defy.'

Kelly and Captain Barclay were impressed with the fine and noble answer that Donnelly gave them. They promised to train him and give him the best advice and expertise at their disposal. While training under Barclay, Donnelly earned his keep by looking after the cows at Calverstown Demense in Kildare. (Donnelly's initials were supposed to have been carved on the rafters at Calverstown House, but there is no sign of them now.)

Dan was to have his first major fight under the patronage of the eccentric Captain Kelly in the Curragh of Kildare. The bout took place on 14 September 1814 in a natural amphitheatre called Belcher's Hollow. Dan was up against a well-known English prize-fighter at the time, Tom Hall, who had been touring the country, teaching and demonstrating the art of boxing. By 1 o'clock there were thousands of people milling around the hollow, which had been roped off.

The art of boxing was very different to what it is now, with no real regard for the safety and wellbeing of the fighters. Fights would carry on until one of or both of the opponents were too weary and injured to continue. There were no rules against dirty tactics and just about anything went in regards to bringing the other man down. Fighters were allowed to jump on each other, bang their opponent's heads off the hard wooden corner posts, hold each other in headlocks, pull hair, ears, noses, etc. It was a vicious and unforgiving sport, and was more like a form of street fighting. The only redeeming thing about it was, unlike today where you have a ten-second countdown, then you were allowed thirty seconds but once they were up, you were out.

For the first part of the fight between Hall and Donnelly, Hall proved to be the stronger opponent and he drew first blood. This was very significant, as bets were made on the basis of who would draw first blood in a bare-knuckle fight. What Hall did not know was that Dan was utilising his trademark tactic of lulling his opponent into a false sense of security and wearing him out at the same time. When Hall realised this and became aware of Donnelly's awesome strength and stamina he began to use a tactic of his own. Every time Donnelly went to deliver a killer blow Hall would drop down on one knee. This would allow him a thirty-second rest. Dan became very aggravated with this cowardly tactic and when Hall went down yet again on one knee, Dan lashed out and caught him on the ear. There was a gush of blood and Hall stated that Donnelly had cheated and should be disqualified. But the onlookers disagreed with Hall. Hall refused to fight on, saying that Donnelly had fouled him but Donnelly was declared the victor. The fight ended in some controversy, but to the Irish people, he was the champion.

After this victory 'Belcher's Hollow' was re-named 'Donnelly's Hollow'. Dan became an Irish champion in having done what so many other Irishmen before him had failed to do: 'stick it to the English oppressors' and live to tell the tale.

After this fight, Dan, fuelled by the admiration and loyalty of his fans, was full of confidence. So sure was he of his fighting ability that he stopped sticking to the strict training programme that Captain Barclay had laid out for him. In fact, he put his time and effort into a completely different activity; enjoying the high life. Dan was to be found in every bar, tavern and inn, being bought drinks and treated like a true superstar. What young man would not love this?

In an effort to curb Dab's drinking, Kelly and Barclay set up a wide circle of spies to keep track on Dan and keep him away from the taverns and bars. Dan eventually realised that Kelly and Barclay had his best interests at heart, so he complied with their regime. He knew, deep down, that the invaders loved to see an Irishman drunk, for that was a great and effortless way to keep him in his place, unable to think or fight for himself. He therefore returned to Dublin where he was greeted with more jubilation. After this Dan went back to work at the carpenters' workshop and resumed some sort of normality.

Dan's reputation as a fighter was to be immortalised in the summer of 1815. That same year Ireland was in a terrible state of affairs and powerless in the face of the mighty British Empire. Britain's navy was the most powerful in the world and its empire was growing stronger and greater by the day. The Duke of Wellington had recently conquered Napoleon Bonaparte at the Battle of Waterloo and Ireland was seen as an embarrassment and a nuisance, a blemish on the well-polished crown of mad old King George III. In fact, Arthur Wellesley, better known as the 1st Duke of Wellington or the Iron Duke, was born in 6 Merrion Street, Dublin in 1769. It was a common occurrence that he would receive jibes and dubious enquiries regarding his Irish birthplace. He would always reply, 'Being born in a stable does not make one a horse'.

It was going to take something or someone spectacular to raise the profile of Ireland and her people. Dan was the man for the job. Dan was their only chance to maintain some respect and dignity. The perfect opportunity for Dan to help his beloved Ireland rise from the ashes of oppression was about to come knocking at his door.

While Dan was working at the carpenters' workshop in Dublin he got word that two men wished to meet him in a local tavern. Something in Dan's bones told him that this was going to be significant, so he agreed.

He went to the tavern and ordered himself a drink; not long after, two unusual-looking men arrived to meet him. One of the men was an African-American who introduced himself as Tom Molineaux. He introduced his comrade as George Cooper. Molineaux explained to Donnelly that they were in Ireland together on an exhibition tour, teaching the art of boxing. Molineaux went on to inform Donnelly that they had been told by a reliable source that he was the best boxer in Ireland and that he would like to challenge him. Donnelly did not answer straight away and he took time to think about the offer. It was a great honour to be sought out by such great fighting men, but Donnelly did not see much of a challenge in Molineaux as he had already been beaten by Cooper. Donnelly told him he did not wish to fight a con-quered man but he was willing to challenge Cooper if he was up for it. Molineaux was angered by this dismissive answer and began to insult Donnelly, calling him all sorts of terrible names. Cooper intervened to calm his comrade and happily agreed to Donnelly's challenge by shaking his hand. Sadly, Molineaux fell into a deep decline after this; he felt that a fight with Donnelly would have helped his profile – which was far from impressive. He had already been beaten by Tom Cribb for the English title and then defeated at the hands of

Cooper. Molineaux already had a serious drink problem and the demons of his time as a slave on a Virginia Plantation, combined with defeat and rejection, proved to be too much. He fell ill while touring the west of Ireland in 1818 and died from liver failure at 34 years of age.

Dan's supporters were delighted to hear that he was going into the ring with Cooper. A native of Stone in Staffordshire, Cooper was a formidable fighter with a fierce reputation and was fondly known amongst the Fancy as 'The Bargeman', because he worked as a labourer on the canal barges. He was of gypsy origin and was rated as one of the greatest prize-fighters of his time. Cooper would punch hard and fast with both fists and he was renowned for his 'one-two' technique, as well as being an expert at blocking and countering punches. Bill Richmond, an African-American pugilist who settled in England, said he was, 'the best natural fighter I have ever worked with'. The one thing that stood against Cooper as a fighter was his contempt for training. Then again, Donnelly was not overly enthusiastic about training either. He claimed he was doing well by limiting himself to just twenty-five glasses of whiskey a day in preparation for a fight. Although this was a far-fetched boast, Donnelly did prefer the taverns to the training ground. Kelly and Barclay made sure that Dan was kept on close watch and made sure he trained well. And Donnelly always complied in the end, for he knew that it was all for the greater good and he was determined to beat Cooper.

The fight was to take place on 13 December 1815 at the now newly christened Donnelly's Hollow at the Curragh of Kildare, the same place where Dan had beaten Hall. On the day of the fight there was an estimated 20,000 people from all over the country gathered to witness this historic event. The air was filled with excitement and fervour as bets were placed and

Cooper was the favourite to win with odds of 10 to 1. It seemed that the Curragh of Kildare was the only place to be.

But George Cooper did not hold the same enthusiasm for the day. Not only was he made to feel unwelcome by the baying crowd but he was bamboozled by the organisers. Cooper had originally been told that the winner received £100 and the looser £20, but not enough cash was raised and now the victor would only receive £60 and the looser nothing at all. Cooper stated that he would not go through with the fight and sat for an hour while the organisers discussed the matter with him. There was a fear of a riot breaking out if the fight was cancelled and when Cooper realised he was up against 20,000 furious Irish people on their own turf, he thought it wiser to just fight the one man as originally intended and the bout went ahead.

Cooper arrived in the ring to polite applause but when Sir Dan made his appearance the roar and applause from the throngs of people could be heard for miles around.

The fight began with some basic sparring and then Donnelly landed the first punch to Cooper's neck. This was greeted by great cheers from the crowd. In retaliation Cooper applied what was known as 'the cross-buttock move'. This was a wrestling tactic and involved getting in front of Dan, throwing him over his hip and sending him crashing to the ground, winding him severely.

By the fifth round Dan was looking like he was going to lose. However, it was at this point that 'Miss Kelly', Captain Kelly's sister, intervened. She told him that she had put her entire fortune on the fight and would be left penniless and destitute if he lost. This appealed to Dan's chivalrous nature and he found the strength to carry on. It was also said that Miss Kelly slipped him a piece of sugar cane to replenish his strength. As she did this she was supposed to have uttered these words: 'Now my charmer, give him a warmer!' After this, the waning Dan revamped his mettle and the fight started to go in his favour.

By the seventh round Dan was fighting well and landed Cooper on the ground with an unmerciful jab. He then jumped on his chest, winding the poor English fighter beyond what seemed like any possible recovery. But Cooper did come back; he was a beast of a man and seemed truly unbeatable. But in the eleventh round, after twenty-two minutes of ferocious battling, Donnelly broke Cooper's jaw with a powerful punch and took him out. The fight was declared finished and Dan declared the overall champion. The cheers from the crowd could be heard for miles around as the people hailed the 'King of the Curragh'.

After the fight Dan marched up the hill to his carriage, some of the ecstatic fans ran behind him and dug with their bare hand at the footprints he left in his wake. The footprints are still there today, leading from the monument erected in his honour at Donnelly's Hollow, and are known as 'The Steps to Strength and Fame'. People regularly visit the site and can walk in the footsteps of Dan Donnelly.

Once Dan was in his carriage he ordered the driver to take him straight home to Dublin and not to hang around for the celebrations in Kildare. This was because he had squandered all his winnings after the last fight, and it had left him penniless. But when he arrived in Dublin there was a huge welcome for him. He was taken around the taverns of Dublin to celebrate his victory. The most outstanding part of these celebrations lay with his mother. As Donnelly was carried through the streets of Dublin on the shoulders of his adoring fans, his mother led the procession with one of her breasts bared. She slapped it and exclaimed, 'There's the breast that suckled him; there's the breast that suckled him!'

After the fight, Dan's winnings of £60 only lasted five weeks. He realised that he needed steady work, as fighting was an unpredictable and dangerous way to earn a crust and popularity did not keep food on the table.

Dan was offered a very attractive career as a publican by a wealthy timber merchant, more than likely his boss at Connery's timber yard. Although there were many pubs in Dublin it seemed like a good business move to have a famous sportsman as the landlord. Dan's tavern was on Poolbeg Street, near Townsend Street where he grew up. The bar was so busy that the staff had no time for breaks in the first three months of it opening. Dan married the girl that he had been courting for a long while and she helped run the bar, while his mother took care of the kitchen. As far as getting back into the ring was concerned, Donnelly vehemently declared that he had no interest at all, for now his place was as a good husband and businessman. However, Donnelly's heavy drinking and constant disappearance started to take their toll. He was squandering money and when he was not present, the punters who came to see him went to the other bars which he frequented, taking their business with them. Dan's poor wife and mother were left to run the show and they were too busy and physically incapable of stopping non-payers and troublemakers. The business suffered and it was not long before it fell away and Dan was left in debt and despair. The only way out was to return to the ring.

However, Dan's reputation as a fierce fighter frightened potential English contenders from coming over to Ireland to fight him and Cooper stated that an English fighter would be made to feel very unwelcome by the Irish mob. He assured them that they would do all in their power to make sure that their man won. This meant that Dan would have to go over to England to fight, which was something that he did not want to do.

He made a few more failed attempts to run bars, but all he did was run up more debt. In the end he succumbed and went to England for fight his third and final fight on 21 July 1819. He defeated Tom Oliver in thirty-four rounds on English turf, at Crawley Down in Sussex. After this final victory Dan stayed on in England, spending all but £20 of his winnings. As he left to return to Dublin he was stopped by a bailiff and handed a writ for £18, for money he owed to Jack Carter, an old sparring partner. He left with just £2 to his name.

There is a famous story of how Dan almost became a knight. After his win against Crawley, he met with Prince Regent, later to become King George IV. When introduced, the Prince stated, 'I am glad to meet the best fighting man in Ireland'. Dan replied, 'I am not that your Royal Highness but I am the best in England'. The Prince was very amused by this and took an instant liking to the brash young Irishman, bestowing a knighthood on him there and then. There is no hard evidence of this but it is a great story and he was fondly known as Sir Dan by his followers and some of the decadent dandies amongst the Fancy who respected his ability as a pugilist.

On 18 February 1820 Dan Donnelly died in his own pub, Pill Lane Public House. This was the only tavern he had left. A few days earlier he complained of feeling 'dull and heavy' but he just put it down to playing football and having a cold. He decided to take a stroll, thinking some fresh air would make him feel better. But this proved too strenuous for him. He was shivering and weak and returned to the tavern and went to bed. His wife was very worried to see how much his condition had worsened by the time she locked up for the night. The next day she called the doctor, who said that Dan was in a fatal condition. She would not believe this because her Dan was stronger than any other man in the land; he had never been sick before or if he was he would never show it nor complain. However, Dan had not taken care of himself; he drank to excess and would not eat food for days, only consuming whiskey and porter. He would sleep outdoors in the rain and on hard stone floors of cellars and barns if he was too drunk to make it home. It was also said that Dan had exerted himself with hard training and drank so much 'water' that he had suffered from 'Hyper-Hydratio', a form of water intoxication.

The night before his death, Dan went into convulsions and his wife asked him if she should get a priest. Dan agreed. The priest came and gave him the last rites. At one o'clock in the morning on Saturday 18 February 1820 Dan died in his weeping wife's arms. According to Patrick Myler's book *Regency Rouge, Dan Donnelly his Life and Legends* (O'Brien Press, 1976), Dan's last words to his wife were: 'I have been given so much and I have done so little'. He was only one month shy of his 32nd birthday when he died. Despite his self-depreciating last words, Dan Donnelly will always be remembered as a hero of the Irish people.

In 1979 a Blue Plaque was erected in Pill Lane, Dublin, commemorating the place of his death. In the Curragh of Kildare a stone obelisk was erected in 1888 in the centre of Donnelly's Hollow with the immortal words 'DAN DONNELLY BEAT COOPER ON THIS SPOT 13 DECEMBER 1815' in relief text on the stone surface.

Dan was buried for a brief period in the ancient 'Bully's Acre' cemetery in Kilmainham, Dublin, but his body was dug up by graverobbers and sold to an unscrupulous surgeon named Hall. The surgeon removed the corpse's right arm and returned the rest of the body for reburial.

Dan Donnelly was only one of many victims of the body-snatchers. Judging by a report published in *The Lancet* in 1830, Bully's Acre was a playing field for the students of Dublin's medical schools:

> An abundant supply is obtained from the burial ground … there is
> no watch on this ground and the subjects are to be got with great
> facility.

Eventually the arm was preserved in red lead paint and sent to a medical college in Edinburgh, Scotland. Here it was used by students to study how the human arm operated. The arm then somehow ended up in a Victorian freakshow, travelling round Britain as part of a circus.

In the early twentieth century it finally got back to Ireland and it became the property of a Belfast bookmaker called Hugh 'Texas' McAleavy in 1904, who displayed it in his pub. McAleavy fell out of love with the macabre exhibition and had it put in his pub's attic where he told his staff not to enter as Donnelly's ghost was there. Eventually Dan's arm got back to Kildare, to the town of Kilcullen, in the 1950s, where it remained on show for forty-three years in the Hideout pub, which belonged to Jim Byrne. He decided to recreate the fight between Donnelly and Cooper at the Hollow in the Curragh.

The arm then travelled to America, where it went on display and then ended up in the Ulster American Folk Museum in Omagh Northern Ireland. It then found its way to the GAA Museum in Croke Park, Dublin, before returning home again. The arm is a grisly shadow to what was once the larger-than-life character Sir Dan Donnelly. Legend has it that he had the longest arms of any boxer and his reach was colossal.

One thing we know for sure, despite Dan's roguish and wayward sensibilities, he had the heart of a lion. When Ireland's people were at their lowest and there seemed to be nothing left to raise their broken spirits, Dan Donnelly stood up and gave the country a sense of pride and integrity that was thought to have died out with the ancient warriors of Erin.

Crawley Common's the place, and who chanced to be there,
Saw an Irishman all in his glory appear,
With his sprig of shillelagh and shamrock so green.
When in sweet Dublin city he first saw the light,
The midwife he kicked, put the nurse in a fright,
But said they, upon viewing him belly and back,
'He's the boy that will serve them all out with a whack,
From his sprig of shillelagh and shamrock to green'.

He thought about fighting before he could talk,
And instead of a go-cart, he first learned to walk,
With his sprig of shillelagh and shamrock so green,
George's Quay was his school, the right place for good breeding,
Where the boys mind their stops, if they don't mind their reading;
There Dan often studied from morning till dark,
And could write, but for shortness, like making his mark,
With his sprig of shillelagh and shamrock so green.

At his trade, as a chip, he was choice in his stuff,
None pleased him but what was hard, knotty and tough,
Like his sprig of shillelagh and shamrock so green,
Nor to strip for his work would he ever refuse,
And right hand and left he the mallet could use,
Length and distance could measure without line or rule,

And a flooring was famous without any tool
But his sprig of shillelagh and shamrock so green.

Whenever he arrogance happened to meet,
No matter in whom, he took out the conceit,
With his sprig of shillelagh and shamrock so green.
To the best of all nations that crossed Dublin bar,
Dan was ready at tipping a mill or a spar,
The hot-headed Welshmen served out by the lot
And cut up their leeks small enough for the pot,
With his sprig of shillelagh and shamrock so green.

Hall and Cooper went over with wonderful haste,
On the soil where it grew, they were longing to taste
Of the sprig of shillelagh and shamrock so green.
On the plains of Kildare 'twas proposed they should meet
And Donnelly wished to give both a good treat;
Yet so such things as Hall, gallant Dan never stooped,
But he took the stout Cooper, and Cooper well hooped,
With his sprig of shillelagh and shamrock so green.

And as Irishmen always politeness are taught,
He the visit returned, and to England he brought
His neat sprig of shillelagh and shamrock so green.
With the good-natured stranger the English seemed shy,
And Cooper no more fickle fortune would try;
But at last the game Oliver entered the field
And, though on his own soil, was soon forced to yield
To the sprig of shillelagh and shamrock so green.

With his kind English friends, he'll again just to please them,
Soon meet, and if troubled with money, soon lose them,
With his sprig of shillelagh and shamrock so green,

But if John Bull is wise, he'll from market hang back
And keep all the corn he has good in his sack,
As to him the next season no harvest will bring,
For, like hail, Dan will beat down the blossoms of spring,
With his sprig of shillelagh and shamrock so green.

2

THE WIZARD
EARL OF KILDARE

*When I was a young lad growing up in Kildare, I was always in
and around Maynooth, a small village that is now a booming
satellite town to Dublin city. Standing proudly and forlorn like
a great ruined memory of a majestic past is Maynooth Castle.
I was always fascinated by its grand and spectral structure.
I remember one evening a long time ago now, when I and an
old friend from Maynooth – who has passed away since then –
were staring up at its mighty doorway and over the arch was a
stone carved coat of arms, worn down by centuries of harsh Irish
elements. We could not figure out what the two strange figures
were holding up the coat of arms on either side. They were
not human, but they were not the usual lions or unicorns one
would expect. They resembled almost alien-like creatures. Their
features were so worn away it was almost impossible to decipher
them. Many years later I was to find out that those figures were
a pair of monkeys. I enquired further and was to find out, much
to my amazement and delight, that the castle once belonged to a
mighty wizard. This is his story.*

Gerald Fitzgerald (1525–1585), was the Eleventh Earl of Kildare. His family had owned Maynooth Castle for over 700 years. He was educated in Italy and when he returned to Kildare in 1552 he had developed an interest in medicine, astronomy and metallergy, much to the curiosity of his community. They spied him conjuring and making spells and so they referred to him as the 'Wizard Earl'.

One Midsummer's Eve, Earl Gerald got ready to gather fern seed. It is said that fern seeds can make you invisible but only if they are gathered on Midsummer's Eve, just as the sun is going down, neither a minute before nor a minute after. And you must be very watchful when you are about to gather the seeds, for there are always bodies who will try to do you harm, and they surely will do it, if all your wits and mind are not on your purpose. For this reason you must be completely alone when you are gathering the fern seed.

The ferns grew at the top of the Hill of Allen and the earl made sure that he arrived there at the right minute on Midsummer's Eve. He had all his wits and all his mind in harness and he was ready to say his spell:

Oh! fern seed
I hold on high
Let me go unseen
To mortal eyes.

Well now! It was then he saw heads popping up behind every stone and rock on the hillside. The country people had expected his arrival and were there to watch all he did.

The earl was furious and if he had had a sword with him he would have sliced off many heads. But you may not carry iron or steel with you on Midsummer's Eve amongst the enchantments, for it is sure to break any spell. So the wizard carried no sword, but he changed into a mighty stag with high and wide antlers and stood menacing the people, sending them running and screaming in all directions.

But it was now too late for the earl to gather the fern seed. He changed back into himself again and went down the hillside, mounted his horse and made the long journey home to his castle.

When he got there he went into a secret chamber, where he sat and read by the light of a magic lamp. He was reading a book of deep magic that was propped up before his eyes, when there was a knock on his chamber door. He opened the door and there stood his young countess.

'I wanted to see what your secret chamber is like, Gerald,' said the countess.

The earl was reluctant to let her in as there were jars filled with things in the chamber that he did not want her to see – terrible things! 'Yes my sweet love,' replied the earl, 'but I was just on my way out onto the tower to look at the night sky.'

'Will you please take me up with you Gerald and tell me the names of all the stars,' asked the countess.

'Of course my sweet love,' replied the earl.

They walked up the winding stairs and out onto the top of the tower. Behind them followed Colgan, the castle's monkey. It was thought by the villagers that Colgan was there to assist the earl with his wizardries but this was not so. A monkey was kept at Maynooth Castle for the reason that a monkey had saved the life of an infant heir. The place had caught fire and the child was trapped in a burning room. The monkey grabbed the infant and jumped onto a tree outside, rescuing the child from the flaming room.

Ever since then there was always a monkey living at the castle – and there are two monkeys on the Fitzgerald coat of arms to this very day.

When the earl and his lady reached the top of the tower, they looked down and saw bonfires blazing on every side. There was shouting and clamouring coming from the country people who were driving their cattle through the fires to free themselves from the evil spirits that they felt sure were upon them after they had witnessed the earl change into a stag.

The earl laughed at their foolish, ignorant ways and he and his lady looked up from the fires and gazed at the sky that was dotted with beautiful, bright stars. The earl pointed out the constellations, the North Star, the planets and told his countess wondrous stories about the heavens.

As he spoke to her he remembered that he hadn't given her much of his company since they were wedded, because his wizardries had taken up his days and nights. But now he would forget them for a while and devote his time to his beautiful wife.

His lover looked at him and told him that she would never really know him.

'Why do you say such a thing?' asked the earl.

'Because you can change into so many shapes, as soon as I know you in one, you change into another!'

'How do you know this my sweet love?' asked the earl.

'The country folk have seen you do it and I have heard it from the servants. You frighten the people terribly, you wicked-shape-shifter!' she said playfully.

'I should frighten them more. I wish I could leave them all speechless!' roared the earl.

'But how will I ever get to know you in all your shapes Gerald?'

'You need know me only in one my love.'

She begged and pleaded with him to change shape. Then the earl spoke softly: 'My love the people say that I can

change into a thousand different shapes, but the truth is I can only change into three.'

'Oh! Let me see them,' she pleaded, and she swore she would never ask him again.

With a heavy heart the earl agreed. He looked at her in a way that he had never done before, which made her shiver. He told her that if anyone who loved him was ever made afraid by the change, he would disappear and no mortal soul would ever see him again.

'Where would you disappear to?' asked the countess.

'I would have to go to the fairy mounds, where I would live for hundreds of years. Mortals would never see me again, except on Midsummer's Eve. I am very much afraid that you will be afraid of the changes,' he said to his wife.

'You could never make me afraid. I would know it was you no matter what you changed into,' replied the countess. She held his face in her hands and kissed him ever so gently. 'Show me,' she whispered.

The earl made her promise not to be frightened and he stood back from her.

She watched in awe as he muttered a spell that made his body twist, turn and shift in all directions as he changed into a great stag with lowered antlers.

'I am not afraid,' she said.

The stag moved away and then changed into the form of a fierce mountain cat with wild staring eyes. She said she was not afraid, but she was, just a little bit. Other accounts state that he turned into a giant serpent that coiled itself around the castle, but this would surely have scared the poor woman half to death.

Then the cat drew back very slowly and, as before, the earl changed back into his own true self.

'And now for the final change! I know you will not be scared of this one,' announced the earl.

He changed before her eyes into a tiny toddler just up to her knee. She was so enchanted by this shape that she cried out to him not to change back for a while. She thought to herself that she loved her husband even more now that he was so small and innocent, especially as she had not been blessed with any children of her own.

But then she screamed out, as the monkey Colgan, who had been hiding in the shadows, suddenly bound forward and lifted the child up into his arms. Hearing her scream he sprang up onto the parapet with the child.

She was terrified and her heart pounded in her breast as she watched the monkey leaping from the tower with the child in its grasp.

There was a terrible moaning sigh as if the night wind had passed over her, carrying with it the earl's spirit.

When Colgan returned there was nothing in his arms. He jumped down from the parapet and crouched in a corner of the room.

The earl had disappeared! She ran to the stairway calling to the servants who came with torches and searched outside with her to see if the earl had fallen from the tower, but there was no trace of him. He had gone to the fairy mounds.

The young countess grew old and died, and to this day her ghost roams the plains of Kildare searching and calling out for her lost earl. What a cruel trick was played on this poor creature, whose ghost only rests on Midsummer's Eve.

***

Other earls and other countesses lived, grew old and died at Maynooth Castle. But still Earl Gerald lived on in the fairy mounds with the heroes who were to help in the deliverance of the land and he continues to be their leader.

On Midsummer's Eve he rides abroad with a train of horsemen whose steeds wear no shoes. Earl Gerald's horse wears shoes, but they are not of iron, being made of solid silver. And when those shoes are worn thin he will know that the people are ready to take help from him and his army and that it is time for him to come.

One Midsummer's Eve, a man was crossing the Curragh of Kildare and he saw a single rider going towards where a company of riders awaited him. 'Has the time come yet?' they cried and the rider replied, 'Not yet! Not yet!' That was just before the earl's descendant, Lord Edward Fitzgerald, was planning an uprising with his comrade Archibald Hamilton Rowan at Rathcoffey Castle.

The descendents of the same perfidious people who had disturbed the earl's gathering of fern seed knew of the legend of the earl and warned the invaders not to strike against Lord Edward on Midsummer's Eve. And it was these same descendants who warned cruel King Henry not to execute the earl's half-brother, Silken Thomas, on Midsummer's Eve for he might be saved by the Wizard Earl and his troop of riders.

***

One evening a tinker man and a blacksmith were walking through the Bog of Allen. They had been squabbling over who had the heavier pack and who should carry the lighter one, when all of a sudden they were startled by the sound of galloping hooves thundering towards them. They could see a huge team of horses being led by a magnificent-looking man on a great white charger with glittering hooves.

The majestic looking man raised an arm, causing the rest of his company to stand still. He dismounted his steed and asked the blacksmith to look at the shoes to see if they

were worn thin. Sure enough, the shoes were made of pure solid silver and none of them were worn thin and the blacksmith confirmed this and he added he had never seen such a magnificent set of shoes in all his life as a blacksmith. The stranger replied: 'Magnificent to you, but to me they are a terrible curse!' He then asked the tinker man the same question and he could only confirm what his colleague had said.

The rider solemnly thanked the two men and mounted his horse. Then he and his troop of riders disappeared into the night mist.

The two men stood speechless in the bog as the moon's light shone mockingly through the swirling mist on their faces, but their minds were full of rich and magnificent thoughts. For they knew only too well that it was the mighty Wizard Earl of Kildare they had met in the barren plains of the bog on that lonely Midsummer's Eve night.

THE LEGEND OF KILKEA CASTLE

The following poem is a poetical rendering of the story of the Wizard Earl and the pleading of his wife to show her his magic powers, having first asked her not to move or speak. But when he changed himself into a bird and a black cat sprang at it, she could not resist trying to stop it, and so broke the spell.

It takes place at Kilkea Castle, which is located just three miles north-west of Castledermot, County Kildare, near the village of Kilkea. It was another medieval stronghold of the Fitzgeralds, Earls of Kildare.

It is seven years since they last awoke
From their death-like sleep in Mullaghmast,
And the ghostly troop, with its snow-white horse,
On the Curragh plain in Kilkea rode past.
For the lord of Kildare goes forth tonight,
And has left his rest in the lonely rath.
Oh, roughen the road for the silver shoes,
That they wear full soon on his homeward path.

So then to his own he may come again,
With a trumpet blast and his warriors bold,
And the spell that was by his lady cast,
Will pass away as a tale once told.
For dearly she loved her noble lord,
And she wished that no secret from her he kept,
So she begged to know why in chamber small
He watched and toiled while the household slept.
But the Wizard Earl would not tell to her

The secret dark of his vaulted cell,
'For fear,' he said, 'in the human frame
Lets loose the power of farthest Hell.'
But she feared for naught save his waning love,
And at length to hear her wish he bent an ear,
So flood, and serpent, and ghost gave place,
For the lady's heart had shown no fear.

Then her lord to a bird was soon transformed,
That rested its wing on her shoulder fair;
But the lady screamed and swooned away,
When a cat sprang forth from the empty air.
For a woman must fear for the one she loves,
And a woman's heart will break in twain,

When she knows that her hand had struck the blow,
To the man she had died to save from pain.

And thus the Earl must sleep as dead,
'Till the silver shoes of his steed are worn,
By which, every seven years, they say,
To Kilkea and back to the rath he's borne.
And swiftly they pass, that phantom band,
With the Earl on his charger gleaming white,
So we think 'tis the shade of a ghost goes by,
With a shifting beam of the moon's pale light.

3

THE POOKA
HORSE

*I first came across the story 'The Kildare Pooka' in William
Butler Yeats's 1888 publication* Folk and Fairy Tales of the
Irish Peasantry. *In Yeats's collection the story was retold by
Patrick Kennedy (1801-1873) from his own book* Legendry
Fictions of the Irish Celts *(1866). Kennedy was well known
for his collections of Leinster folk tales. At the age of twenty-
one he enrolled in a teacher-training course at the Kildare
Place Society, officially known as The Society for Promoting the
Education of the Poor of Ireland. In 1822 he was appointed as
a teacher there. He gave up teaching at some point and opened a
lending-library and bookshop in Dublin.*

*What is very strange about Kennedy's story is that he removed
all the names of places, characters and buildings from the text,
leaving only the first letter of each word followed by a dash.
Growing up in Rathcoffey, I was told by an old-timer that
Rathcoffey Castle had its own ghost or 'Pooka' residing there
and so I suspected that the missing name in Kennedy's story was
Rathcoffey Castle, but I had no proof.*

*The word 'Pooka' simply means 'ghost' or 'phantom' in the
Irish language. The Pooka is a solitary and sinister fairy who has
most likely never appeared in human form. His shape is usually*

that of a horse, bull, goat, eagle or donkey. But most commonly he appears as a horse, and derives great delight from taking unwary riders on his back and transporting them over ditches, rivers and mountains, before shaking them off in the early grey-light of the morning.

I had heard stories about phantom horses in Kildare many times, as Kildare is famous for its horse breeding and lots of people I knew at the time kept horses.

I first heard the name Pooka being used by the other children when I was growing up to describe 'trick or treating' at Halloween. 'Are going on the Pooka?' they would ask you coming up to Halloween.

Many years later by sheer chance I came across a collection called Irish Fairy Tales *by the Irish historian and folklorist Padraic O'Farrell, published by Gill & Macmillan in 1997. And there it was, 'The Rathcoffey Pooka', and the missing names were filled in! I was so excited; all I had heard and suspected had been true. And now I would like to share this story in all its glory with you. It is one of my favourites, and like all the stories in this collection I have put my own twist on the tale.*

In the province of Leinster lies County Kildare and within that county lies Rathcoffey in the civil parish of Balraheen. Halfway between Maynooth and Clane, and standing on top of Rathcoffey Hill, is Rathcoffey Castle. The castle is now in ruins but it was once a magnificent building, renowned for its feasts and banquets. There are two parts to Rathcoffey Castle: the remains of the twelfth-century Norman castle, built by the Wogan family and the shell of Rathcoffey House, built by Archibald Hamilton Rowan in 1784.

Rowan was a prominent figure in the 1798 Rebellion. In 1790 he was a founding member in Dublin of the

Society of United Irishmen, working alongside such famous revolutionaries as William Drennan and Theobald Wolfe Tone. His involvement in these activities left him in a lot of bother. To put it another way, he was what you might call a wanted man. On one occasion he was hiding out at Rathcoffey House when he saw a troop of English soldiers riding towards him over the hill. Archibald did not waste any time, for he knew these boys were not calling around for a cup of tea and a chat. So he went out onto the balcony of his house and whistled out for his horse, which came galloping out from his stable beside the house. Archibald jumped off the balcony, landing square on the horse's back and away they rode towards Clongowes Wood Castle, which was known at the time as Castlebrowne. His pursuers were hot on his trail, firing their muskets at him. He rode like the devil towards Castlebrowne and when he got there he burst through the front doors and straight up the stairs. He opened the windows of one of the top rooms and threw his hat out. His pursuers were close behind and followed him up to the room and saw the open window and his hat lying on the ground so they figured he had jumped out to escape. They ran back down the stairs and searched everywhere for him, but there was neither sight nor sound of him.

What his tormentors did not know was that there was a secret chamber in one of the top-floor rooms of the castle. Archibald pressed a hidden button in one of the bookcases and this opened a secret door and in he went to join his dear friend Wogan Browne for a glass of fine wine and a game of cards, while enjoying a good laugh at his pursuers' expense. That secret room is still there to this day, along with the hidden button that opens the door.

However, the most famous story surrounding Archibald concerns his home. Every night, after all the merriment was over and all the crockery and cooking ware was left in the kitchen to be washed, the sound of banging and clattering accompanied by the sound of hysterical laughter and whistling could be heard coming from the kitchen. The servants were all scared out of their wits and never dared enter the kitchen to discover the sources of the sound. And every morning, to their amazement, the kitchen was always found spotless and everything clean and in its place. You could have eaten your dinner off the floor it was so well scrubbed.

Now there was a young scullery boy who lived and worked at the castle and he was a very lazy boy. He was so lazy that the only time he would lift his hand to do something was when he wished to scratch his head or pick his nose. He was so lazy that he made his mother cry. Now Rathcoffey Castle was a great place for a boy like this to work in, as he never had to do a stroke. It was heaven altogether, and why should he do anything when whatever it was coming to the kitchen at night was doing such a fine job, far better than he could ever do himself?

Well, one night, out of curiosity and boredom, he decided to see who or what was making all the noise and doing all the cleaning. He waited until all the ware was brought into the kitchen and left piled high to the ceiling with the mice eatin' away at them. He knew that no one would bother him as they were all to frightened to go into the kitchen after dark so he built himself a nic big fire in he fireplace and lay down on some cushions before the hearth. Ah! It was a grand fire indeed. He could feel the warmth of the flames against his face, smell the aromatic smoke as it curled up the chimney, the flames throwing shadows on the walls like dancing demons and he was eased into a deep sleep by the gentle sound of the crackling wood.

Then, all of a sudden, he was woken by the most terrible howling and shrieking. Then the words 'I've got ya now ya boy ya! I've got ya now!' were bellowed into his face. The boy looked up in terror and standing above him was a great black horse with red eyes like burning coals and steam hissing out of its curled nostrils.

'Whooo are you?' stammered the boy, his heart pounding with fear. The horse grinned at him, revealing two rows of ivory white teeth. There was a glint of menace in the creature's eye that sent a shiver down the boy's spine.

The horse pulled over a chair and sat down in it and crossed his legs. He then reached in to his big black mane and produced a large clay pipe. He lit the pipe, took a deep drag out of it and exhaled the thick smoke out his nostrils. Then cleared his throat and spat onto the fire, causing it to hiss like an angry serpent. And then the horse began ...

'I am the Pooka horse and I dwell amongst the ruins and the hilltops. I have been driven monstrous by much solitude and they say I am of the race of the nightmare! But I was once a boy like you, a lazy boy just like you!' The Pooka horse looked ever so pleased with himself as he went on to tell the poor boy his story. 'I was so lazy, I made my mother cry and the fairies were so angry with me they sent a big black Pooka Horse, who threw me on his back and ran the full length and breadth of Ireland with me holding on for dear life. He ran to the south, where he took me to the top of Mount Carrantuohill in the County Kerry and he howled like a wolf. Then he took me to the west, where my teeth chattered as his hooves clattered across the mighty Burren in the County Clare. Then he took me to the north, where he jumped across Maggie's Leap in the County Down and finally he brought me to the east, where my heart pounded as he bounded across the plains of the

Curragh of Kildare. He came to a sudden halt and I was sent flying into the furze bushes and when I came to I was no longer a boy but the great black Pooka horse that you see before you now.'

The creature went on to explain that there was a curse upon him. 'I would remain a Pooka horse and travel the land seeking out lazy people and when I found them, I would have to carry out all their chores and labour. The only way to break the spell is that I must find a boy or a girl lazier than I was, and catch them sleeping when they should be working.' The Pooka grinned menacingly at the boy and took a deep drag from his pipe. He went on, 'I found you a long time ago boy, dossing about, skiving off your duties and playing truant. All I had to do was to catch you sleeping. I waited and worked here doing all your chores and now I got ya! Ha!' roared the Pooka horse.

'Please!' begged the boy. 'Please give me one last chance. I promise I will never be lazy again and I will do all that is asked of me and more.' The Pooka horse leered down at the boy and curled back his lips in a snarl, revealing those terrible teeth. Hissing at the boy he said, 'We'll see, we'll see ...' With that, the Pooka put out his pipe, pushed it back into his mane, stood up, turned and opened the door. The boy heard him galloping across the plain outside, crying 'We'll see! We'll see!'

The poor lad jumped up and began to scrub, mop and wash everything in the kitchen. He did this every day and night for a brave long while. And there was no sign of the Pooka horse. The people of Rathcoffey Castle were very pleased with and proud of their scullery boy, and they rewarded him well and he had a day off every week to do as he pleased. And they were no longer full of fear at night with all that strange commotion going on in the kitchen.

As time went on, the boy began to think that the Pooka horse was a thing of the past. In fact, he started to believe that he imagined the whole experience. He had been working so hard, far harder than anyone else in the castle and he deserved a night off. He was due a holiday the following week, but he could not wait.

So one night, after the festivities were over and all the dirty dishes were brought into the kitchen, he went inside as before and built himself a large fire. Ah! How lovely it was! He needed a rest and this was well-deserved.

It was not long before he drifted off to sleep, snoring away contentedly ...

'Ahhhhhhh! Ha! Ha! I got you now for sure, ya boy ya!' The boy jumped out of his sleep absolutely terrified, his heart beating in his breast.

Standing above him was the Pooka horse. He grabbed the boy in his arms and roared with laughter in his face, then dropped the boy to the floor. The boy gawked in disbelief as the monster turned back into human form and he watched as his own body began to cover with hair and his hands turn to hooves. Standing before him was a young man looking ever so pleased with himself. Then he turned and ran from the house singing out 'I'm free! I'm free!'

The scullery boy had become a Pooka horse and was doomed to search the land for a boy or a girl lazier than him to lift the terrible curse. But he could not bring himself to punish a child in such a dreadful way. So instead he went about helping the poor, weak and the sick. He helped wherever he could and never slacked on any job he started. He did all this without anyone knowing who did it or receiving any thanks. Then one day, many years later, the curse was lifted and he was no longer a boy, but a young man. And he then travelled from house to house, school to school telling young

people his story, warning them of what might happen if they were lazy. But somewhere out there roams another Pooka horse who is keen to pass the curse on to someone else. So be wary and diligent in your work, for he might come looking for you!

4

THE RACE OF
THE BLACK PIG

*An ancient trackway across the Curragh was known as the Race of
the Black Pig or the Black Ditch. This ancient track, some twenty
miles in length, was the source of many traditional folk tales.*

There was once a great schoolmaster who lived in Kildare a
long time ago. Like the Wizard Earl of Kildare, he had some
truly magnificent powers. One of his favourite tricks was
to turn his students into pigs. One day they were all playing
in the field beside the schoolhouse, in the form of black pigs,
having a great time altogether and it just so happened that
Thomas Fitzgerald, the Tenth Earl of Kildare – better known
as Silken Thomas – was hunting in that area with a pack of
hounds and an entourage of other noblemen. Seeing the pigs
in the field, he set the pack of hounds on them. The poor pigs
all ran in different directions through the countryside, and by
doing this they formed the dykes called the Black Pig Dykes
which are to be seen throughout the country. Another version
of the story is that when the schoolmaster saw his students
being terrorised by the hounds he himself turned into a great
black boar and chased the dogs, carving up ditches and dykes
with his ferocious tusks.

Another story talks about a king from the north of Ireland who employed a schoolmaster for the education of his two sons. This same king was notorious for his knowledge in sorcery and magic, and he possessed mighty powers. On one occasion, during his absence at a hurling match, the schoolmaster and his two pupils entered the king's private room, though they had been forbidden to enter it under any circumstances.

On a table lay a great book of magic and this the schoolmaster opened and he began to read aloud from its pages, though he could not understand the meaning of what he had read. After a short time he happened to look up from the book, and was amazed to see that, in place of his two pupils, two great shaggy hounds were sitting there, looking at him. With sheer fright, he ran from the room as fast as he could. When the wizard king returned home that evening, he was met near the castle by two strange hounds that he had never seen before, but they were delighted to see him and wished to be at his side at all times.

In a state of bewilderment the king marched to his room, and on seeing the open book, guessed what had occurred. In a fit rage he sent for the schoolmaster, who was hiding somewhere in the castle. He approached the wizard king sheepishly. Despite his remorse, the king changed him into a big black boar and then drove him from the castle with a great blackthorn stick. He set the two hounds on him and the boar fled for its life. Crossing the River Boyne, it ran through County Meath, then to Maynooth in County Kildare, on through Kildare into the County Carlow, then away through the country lying between the rivers Barrow and the Slaney, until it reached Priestshaggard in the County Wexford, where the two hounds eventually killed the unfortunate boar. The hounds then returned home and were transformed by the king back into their human form.

But the race that had taken place had torn up so many ditches and dykes that they too were named after the black pig.

The following is another great story about the black pig that was collected by Mario Corrigan, who has been a great help in writing this book. It tells the tale of how a Kildare shepherd called Bartle Dunnigan was looking after his flock on the Curragh one winter. The place was covered in thick snow and Dunnigan was relaxing and puffing on his pipe when he heard his dog barking like mad. He reckoned that one of his sheep must have got stuck in the snow, so he went to rescue it. To his amazement, when he arrived at the place where the dog was barking, he did not find a sheep but a little man with his head stuck in the mound of snow, legs kicking in all directions. Dunnigan looked at the creature in astonishment, wondering what he was doing and how he had not caught his death of cold in such wild conditions. The little man freed himself from the pile of snow, wiped his face with a red handkerchief and stated that is was hot work indeed looking for Bartle Dunnigan, and how it was that he had not found him until now. Dunnigan replied that he had never known the strange little man and he must have mistaken him for someone else. But it was odd that he did know his name. The tiny man said that he had important business to conduct with Dunnigan and the poor shepherd wondered what sort of business he could possibly have with him.

The strange little man said that before he could disclose the nature of the business he would like a blast of Dunnigan's pipe. He took a good drag and commented on the quality of the tobacco. He then spoke about people in Dunnigan's life from a long time ago when he was a boy. He then told Bartle that the reason he had his head in the snow was a penance he had to do as a result of a misdeed. He explained that he would have to do it for five hours every three days before Christmas for all eternity. Old Bartle was frightened by this and stood back, stating that the little man must be a right devil. The man told him it was of no importance what sins he had committed, for he was paying for them now and he told Dunnigan about other poor souls who had far worse penance than he had and they were harmless enough creatures.

He then explained that his penance was for a wrong he had done to Dunnigan's great-grandfather. You see, he had intended to buy a suckling pig from Bartle's great-grandfather on a fair day. But when the grandfather had his back turned the man made off with the pig without paying for it. Everyone related to Bartle's great-grandfather was dead now, except Bartle himself. So he had to apologise to Bartle before it was too late, because once Bartle was gone there was no one else left to make amends with and then he would be cursed for eternity.

So Bartle saw this as a great opportunity to make a few bob from this wide boy. And he told him that the price of pigs had gone up a lot since his great-grandfather was about. The little man smiled and told him that he could not give him any money but he could give him back the pig the same way he had found it all those years ago. He told him to come to the same spot tomorrow and poke the furze bush he was standing beside with a stick and the pig would walk out. And then he stated that they would be quits and he could relax in the next life. But then he grabbed Bartle and warned him not to speak a word of any of this to a mortal soul or tell where he got the pig from or he would do something terrible to him. He shook his fist at Bartle to make his point and then disappeared.

So the next morning Bartle got up bright and early and made his way to the furze bush, making sure no one was about to witness anything. He had a spancil to tie the pig and a stick to poke the furze. He prodded at the bush but there was no pig. He was about to give up and with one last attempt he called the pig and sure enough it called back with three grunts. He was calling away when he heard a voice asking him what was he doing and who he was calling out to? He looked around and standing there was Jack Joyce a local lad. 'Oh! Nothing,' replied Bartle in the most calm way he could manage, so as not to blow his cover. Joyce asked him then why was he prodding the furze for the last hour and Bartle had to think on his feet. He replied that he thought he saw a weasel run into the bush and he was trying to scare him out.

With this the pig snorted loudly three times and Joyce stated that it must be a queer weasel indeed. So Joyce offered to help. With that the pig, a fine specimen too, bolted out of the bush and the two boys went running after it. Bartle tripped on some thistles and Joyce grabbed at the pig, thinking it was his now. Bartle was not happy that this little brat was trying to take his property. The pig wriggled free but then stopped to turn up the grass with his nose and Bartle saw this as his chance. But Joyce ran at it and the pig was off again. The pig ran inside the house of a Mrs Donegan and the two boys came running after it. Mrs Donegan closed the door and stood at the threshold. The two boys started protesting, both saying that the pig was theirs but Mrs Donegan stated no one would get the beast until she knew the identity of the rightful owner.

It just so happened that two policemen came along the road and Mrs Donegan was sure this would solve the argument. The sergeant and his comrade took the two lads to the courthouse to settle the matter but the judge stated it was too late and it would have to be tomorrow. In the meantime, he wanted four constables guarding the house with the pig in it.

Word of the dispute spread and when the judge took his seat the next day the courthouse was packed with excited people. Dunnigan was feeling bad and he did not know what to say, for he remembered what the little man had said to him and how he had threatened to do something terrible to him if he said where he had got the pig. To say he found him in the furze meant that Joyce had as much right to him as he did. It was a tough station for Bartle. When the court proceeded, the judge asked Bartle if the pig was his and he agreed it was and the judge asked if he had any witnesses to prove his ownership of the beast. Bartle told the judge that he got the pig from a man he had never met or seen before and did not know him in any way and the man was now gone for good. The judge remarked on how odd this was.

The judge then turned to Joyce and asked him the same question. Joyce claimed the pig as his own, and stated that he bought it fair and square from a widow woman. The judge said that if he could produce this widow woman then the case would be closed and the pig was his. Joyce then went on to say that the widow was an orphan with no family, as they had all met gruesome deaths by misfortune and wild beasts and she had since left for Australia. So there were no witnesses from Joyce either. The judge stated that this was a most remarkable case. He adjourned the court for lunch and there was great excitement indeed.

The case dragged on and the judge was not happy and jury members had to leave to attend to chores and responsibilities. Then the judge stood up and demanded that Bartle be removed from the court.

And when poor Bartle was escorted out, sure that he had lost, the judge turned to Joyce and asked him what was the gender of his pig, male or female. Well Joyce stated that it was a sow, a female. Before Joyce had a chance to say another word he was silenced and Bartle was called back in. As soon as he stepped in the door the judge asked him the same question. What gender was the pig?

He thought hard for he did not know and the judge became very angry with him. But then he figured the little man would have taken a hog for its breeding possibilities.

So he told the judge it was male. Joyce then protested and tried to change his story but the judge silenced him. He then stated that he and some lawmen would go to the house and look at the pig. He then lowered his voice and said that there had been some terrible time-wasting and misuse of the law this day and whoever he found out was lying would pay dearly for their misconduct.

The judge set off for the house of Mrs Donegan and all the people from the courthouse followed him. There was great tension and the judge called for Bartle and Joyce to come with him inside the house. Poor Bartle thought he was done for, facing hanging or thinking that he might be sent to the Cannibal Islands. The woman of the house said the pig was gone and the police said they heard it grunting outside but could not find it. The judge was fit to send the two boys for ten years to the Cannibal Islands, but in the end he was lenient and let them off on the First Offenders Act.

When it was all over Bartle headed for home, when all of a sudden he heard someone whistle at him. It was the tiny man who had appeared to him and got him into all this trouble in the first place. Bartle was furious for the little man was singing away, oblivious to the heartache he had inflicted on him. Bartle went at him with his stick but the little man dodged him and said, 'I want to have a straight chat with ye!' The little man told him he had tried to do him a good turn and told him to say nothing, but instead Bartle had the whole county up in arms. He picked up a snowball and threw it at Bartle, hitting him right between the eyes and almost knocked him out. Bartle then went home and had a hot drink or two to calm his nerves and he tried to tell his wife of his troubles, but she just smiled at him. Ah, the women are a hard bunch to make any understanding of a man's predicaments.

The next day a hollow could be seen where the pig had gone and this was known from then on as the Black Pig's Run. And it is said that every seven years since that day, on the Wednesday night before Christmas, at the stroke of midnight, a black pig can be seen racing along with a tiny man on its back, riding for all he is worth. And that is how the Race of the Black Pig on the Curragh of Kildare got its name. *Sin é an scéal.*

5

SAINT BRIGID

Saint Brigid is the patron saint of Kildare and her symbol is the Saint Brigid's Cross, which appears on the County Kildare crest. Her colour is white and this is the colour worn by the Kildare Gaelic football team and why they are fondly known as the Lily-Whites. Saint Brigid is said to have built the first church in Kildare. It was built out of oak and Kildare translated into Irish is *Cill Dara*, meaning Church of the Oak.

What is really interesting about her character is that she was a pagan goddess before she became a saint and her story as a saint overlaps with a lot of pagan ideals and symbolism. Many of the Saint Brigid's wells around Ireland were originally pagan wells, like the Trinity Well outside Carbury in Kildare. Whether you see her as a saint or a pagan deity, she certainly is the stuff of great folklore.

The name Brigid was originally that of a Celtic goddess meaning the 'The Exalted One', and, like her cross, she made a smooth transition from pagan goddess to Christian saint. She was venerated all over Ireland and, according to legend, was the daughter of Daghda who was a Celtic tribal father-god and the chief to the Tuatha De Danann,

who were to become what is more commonly known as 'The Fairies'. He had great magical ability and was extremely powerful.

Other sources suggest that she was born in AD 443 and died in AD 524 and that her father, Dubhthach, was a pagan chieftain of Leinster and her mother, Brocca, a Christian Pict and slave, who was baptised by Saint Patrick.

Even as a saint, Brigid still possessed all of her mighty godlike powers and she used them well to do her work. She was born in a druid's household and was suckled on the milk from magical cows. When she was older she was able to produce endless quantities of food and produce milk from cows that would have been considered dry. She was always heavily associated with both fertility and animals. She had healing powers and was very compassionate to children and the vulnerable. She also had a great love of music, poetry and the arts.

Her first small church in Kildare town became a centre of religion and learning and the town developed into a cathedral city. She also founded a school of art that specialised in metalwork and illuminated texts. From here was produced *The Book of Kildare*, but it disappeared around the time of the Reformation. It was considered to be as beautiful, if not more, than *The Book of Kells*, which can still be seen in Trinity College Dublin today.

There are many wonderful tales surrounding Saint Brigid and here are a few that I have collected, including a series of short stories from Patrick Kennedy, Lord Walter Fitzgerald of the *Kildare Archaeological Society Journal*.

SAINT BRIGID'S CROSS

The story we were always told about how the cross came to be was based on a tale where Saint Brigid was called to the home of a great Celtic chieftain (there is speculation that it may have been her own father Dubhthach) who was dying. Word was sent to Brigid that she was to go to the deathbed of a pagan chieftain who was full of fear at the prospect of not going to heaven – this wonderful place that he had heard so much about. Brigid did not waste any time and made her way to his abode, where all his servants and warriors were gathered around. When the chieftain saw her, he reached out his hand and asked her to tell him of this man they called Christ and what he had to offer. She told him the story of Our Lord and how he died upon the cross for our sins. The old king was impressed that a man would give up his own life to save the souls of his fellow men and he wanted to be united with a god that would put others before himself.

He had never seen a cross before and said that it would be good to have a full understanding of what it was before he was willing to accept it into what was left of his life. Brigid realised that in her haste she had brought no crucifix with her and then the thought occurred to her that she could make one for him. The mattress that the old man was lying upon was made of rushes, so she grabbed a handful of them and carefully wove a delicate cross from them and presented it to the old king. She then blessed him and baptised him with water and then held his hand as he slipped away.

To this day Saint Brigid's crosses are made all over Ireland, especially by children for Saint Brigid's Day on 1 February. They adorn many houses in Ireland and America, being considered by many as being a very significant symbol of Ireland's transition from paganism to Christianity. They are supposed to protect homes from fire and evil spirits and bring happiness to a household.

Saint Brigid's Cloak

The King of Leinster was not a particularly generous man, and Saint Brigid found it difficult to make him contribute in a respectable fashion to her many charities. One day, when he proved more than usually irritated, she at last said, 'Well, at least grant me as much land as I can cover with my cloak.' To silence her persistent begging he agreed to her request.

They were, at the time, standing on the highest point of ground on the Curragh, and she directed four of her sisters to spread out her cloak. Accordingly they took up the garment, but instead of laying it flat on the turf, each virgin, with face turned to a different point of the compass, began to run swiftly, the cloth expanding in all directions. Other pious ladies, as the border enlarged, seized portions of it to preserve something of a circular shape, and the elastic extension continued till the breadth was a mile at least. 'Oh, Saint Brigid!' said the frightened king, 'what are you about?'

'I am, or rather my cloak is, about to cover your whole province to punish you for your stinginess to the poor.'

'Oh, come, come, this won't do. Call your maidens back. I will give you a decent plot of ground and be more liberal in the future.'

Thus, Saint Brigid gained as much land as she needed to build her monastery. The king and his count were both dismayed and amazed and the king, realising she was blessed by God, became a patron of her monastery, assisting her with money and provisions.

SAINT BRIGID AND THE HARPS

It was not in the nature of things that a Celtic saint should despise music or poetry. Saint Brigid, being once on a journey, sought hospitality for herself and her sisters in the house of a petty king. This king and his chief officers, including his harpers, were absent, but some of his sons did all that religious reverence and a hospitable spirit could devise for the suitable reception of their honoured guests. After a frugal meal the hosts and guests continued an interesting conversation, during which Brigid, observing the harps suspended on the wall, requested the princes to indulge her with some of the ancient melodies of the country. 'Alas, honoured lady!' said the eldest, 'our father and the bard are absent, as we have mentioned, and neither my brothers nor myself have practised the art. However, bless our fingers, and we will do all in our power to gratify you.' She touched their fingers with the tips of her own, saying some prayers in a low voice and when the young men sat down to play the instruments, they drew from them such sweet and powerful melody as was never before heard in that hall. So enthralling was the music that it seemed as if they could never tire of playing, nor their audience of listening. While the performance was still proceeding the king and his suite entered the large hall and were amazed at hearing sweet and skilful strains from the untaught fingers of the princes. Recognising the saint and her ladies, their wonder ceased.

RATHBRIDE AND THE WART STONE

It is said that the ends of Saint Brigid's lands were marked with four large crosses – in other words there were crosses at the four corners of the Curragh. There are no crosses left standing today, but there is a large stone at Rathbride (Brigid's Rath or Rath Bhríde) Cross on the Kildare to Milltown road. It is said that this is the base of an old Christian cross and indeed may have been the base of one of the fabled crosses that marked out Brigid's territory. The stone is rough on top and water gathers in the holes and hollows and locals believed that this stone had miraculous powers. If you suffered from warts then you placed the afflicted area (usually the hand) into the water gathered on top of the stone and you would be cured. I'm sure people would also take the water and apply it to other areas also. This stone is still known as The Wart Stone.

LOUGHMINANE OR LOCH LEAMNACHTA

One day, eighteen bishops came to visit Kildare and Brigid and her nuns had to cater for their needs. Brigid asked her cook Blaithnait if there was enough milk, but Blaithnait said there wasn't as she had already milked the cows. Brigid fell to her knees in prayer and an angel appeared and told her to milk the cows again. When they milked the cows, the milk filled all the tubs they had brought and it is said they could have filled all the vessels in Leinster. The milk spilled over the tops of the vessels and created a loch or lake, which forever after was known as Loch Leamnachta or 'lake of the new milk'.

'THE BREEDOG'

Another fascinating tradition associated with St Brigid is 'The Breedog'. According to Lord Walter Fitzgerald of the Kildare Archaeological Society, there are several traditions all over Ireland associated with it.

'The Breedog' is probably a remnant of the procession in honour of St Brigid, when her statue would be carried about. The rude figure, if we can call it such, goes by the name of Breedog, i.e. *Brigid óig*, Brigid the Virgin.

In County Mayo, the children dress up a figure and decorate it with ribbons and flowers. Then four or more of them carry it from house to house on St Brigid's Day, and ask the housewife to 'honour the Breedog'. One of the girls hums a tune, and the others dance. It is thought a very rude thing to refuse to honour the effigy. Eggs are taken if the housekeeper has no coppers to give. There is a spokeswoman for the party, who has a short speech that she delivers at every house. The money and eggs collected are evenly divided between the girls, who purchase sweets and cakes with the proceeds. The girls usually choose the day for their rounds; then, at night, the boys go round with what is called 'The Cross'. This is a cross made of two ropes; four boys catch an end each, and then they dance away to the music of a flute; like the girls they, too, gather contributions from each house they visit, and spend the result in a jollification.

In County Kerry the 'Breedhogue' is an image, supposed to be St Brigid. It consists of a churn-dash or broomstick, padded round with straw, and covered with a woman's dress, the head being formed of a bundle of hay, rolled into a ball; the hands are formed of furze branches, stuck up in the sleeves. This figure is carried round from house to house by boys and girls on St Brigid's Eve. One boy starts a tune, and the others commence dancing, after which they are given pennies, or more generally eggs, in honour of the 'Biddy'. No matter what the weather is, the Breedhogue is annually carried round, though since moonlighting commenced in Kerry it had to be discontinued for some time, owing to the fear of being mistaken for members of that band.

Walter Fitzgerald recorded the event in County Cork:

> In some parts of the county the boys dress up a female figure in a white dress with gaudy ribbons, which they call 'a Breedhoge'. They are generally themselves queerly dressed and disguised. On St Bridget's Eve they visit from house to house in the parish, particularly those houses where there are young women who, they say, should get married during Shrove time. If they are welcomed, and given money for a spree, then they will praise up and recommend the girls to their male friends; but if not, they will warn them to avoid them.

I myself have seen the Breedog being used on St Brigid's Day in various parts of Northern Ireland. The Breedog that I have seen is made from straw and bound tightly together to make an effigy of a doll. The doll is then dressed in white cloth and adorned in flowers and carried in processions.

6

THE DEVIL AT
CASTLETOWN HOUSE

Growing up in Kildare, I went to school in Celbridge and I was always interested in Castletown House, a big stately home with a strange aura about it. The house was built by William 'Speaker' Conolly (then Speaker of the Irish House of Commons) in 1722. The Conolly family were well-known for building other fine pieces of architecture around Kildare. During the Great Famine they commissioned 'Conolly's Folly' or 'The Obelisk' to generate work for the starving. 'The Wonderful Barn' was also built to store food.

William 'Speaker' Conolly had a hunting lodge built on top of Mount-Pelier Hill in the Dublin Mountains in 1725. After his death in 1729 the lodge lay unused until it was bought by Richard Parsons, Earl of Rose, in 1735. He turned Conolly's lodge into 'The Hellfire Club'. This became a place of demonic practices and extreme debauchery. And, indeed, it is said that Auld Nick himself decided to pay a visit. In fact, it seems that the Devil may have made several visits to Castletown House. I found this story in a great little book called Irish Ghosts *by J. Aeneas Corcoran published by Geddes & Grosset in 2002.*

Castletown House was inherited by William Conolly's nephew, who married Lady Anne Wentworth, daughter of the Earl of Stafford. One day she saw the figure of a tall man standing in the upper gallery, who proceeded to walk down a nonexistent staircase, past a big window, taking little steps as though each stair was quite shallow. He paused and laughed, a high, cold, arrogant laugh, as though he were the rightful owner of the place, mocking the people who lived there.

Ten years later, a staircase was built in exactly the location in which Lady Anne had seen the figure. More than twenty years after that, Lady Anne's son, Thomas Conolly, now the owner of the house, was walking in the garden with his wife, recalling the strange story of what his mother had seen in the hall. A few days after that, he was out riding with the Kildare Hounds. Many of the hunt gave up and went home, for the fox was proving to be tricky and elusive. Only Conolly and a handful of others were left, when he noticed that a newcomer seemed to have joined them. Mounted on a fine black horse that looked as fresh as if it had just come out of the stable door. The rider was a tall fellow, dressed in grey, with great thigh-boots.

'Good day to ye,' called out Conolly. 'A poor day for sport, though.'

The man merely grinned, showing large, discoloured teeth, then set his horse to the slope of the hill and went galloping up. At that same moment, the hounds began to bay, as if they were closing in on their prey. Conolly followed the horseman up the hill, but when he got to the brink, he reined in, astonished. The hounds were not to be seen, but the stranger stood there, dismounted from his horse, and with the bloody carcass of the fox held in both hands high above his head. He grinned again at Conolly, then lowered the fox's

body to the level of his mouth, and in one swift bite with his great teeth, cut away the brush. Dropping the carcass he held it out to Conolly, still grinning.

The young squire of Castletown turned away in disgust, but the man then spoke: 'Conolly, if you will not take the brush, will you offer me a cup of something hot in your great house?'

The Conollys had always maintained a tradition of hospitality, and Thomas did not refuse, though there was something about the man, his leering smile, and his high voice, that turned his blood. 'There is hot rum punch at my house for all who want it,' he said.

The stranger entered the house at Conolly's side. Conolly saw him pause and survey the great entrance hall, and the staircase that came sweeping down from the gallery, past the window, and he heard a sound of hissing laughter escape from the man's lips. The stranger took a chair by the fire, and stretched out his legs, but when a servant came up, to help take his riding boots off, he waved the man away.

'Leave me be,' he said. 'I am sleepy and don't choose to be disturbed.'

He closed his eyes and appeared to settle down for a comfortable nap. Coming more closely to get a good look at him, Conolly was amazed to see that the stranger was as hairy as an animal. Coils of hair matted on the backs of his hands and more emerged at his cuffs. Tufts of coarse hair sprang from his ears. Beginning to have suspicions, Conolly told two of the servants to take off one of the sleeping stranger's boots. As they cautiously worked it off, a thickly haired leg appeared, terminating in a great black hairy hoof.

Hastily, as all the company retreated from the fire, Conolly sent a man to ride for the parish priest. As the priest arrived, the stranger awoke, glanced at his feet and saw one boot had been removed. With a snarl he rose up, and placed himself against the mantelpiece, right in front of the roaring fire, and laughed the same high-pitched, spine-chilling laugh that Lady Anne had heard all those years ago in the same room. The priest, as terrified as anyone, mumbled an incantation, but it had no effect except to provoke further demoniac laughter. At last, the priest in desperation threw his missal at the figure. It missed its target and struck the mirror above the fireplace, which shattered. But, at the threat of being touched by the holy book, the figure leapt high in the air and vanished, leaving only a greasy boot in the room, and a great crack in the stone fireplace.

The Story of Castletown House in Celbridge

This is another version of the story given to a young person at Rathcoffey School over eighty years ago by John Brilly of Rathcoffey, Donadea. He had heard it several times from the old people around him. This story was collected by The Irish Folklore Commission in University College Dublin.

There was a gentleman living in Castletown House, Celbridge named Conolly. He was a very bad and wicked man. One morning he was going out to hunt. As he was mounting his horse, he said he would ride against the devil or get the fox's brush.

On leaving his own house a strange gentleman saluted him and accompanied him to the Liffey Bridge at Celbridge, where the hounds met and from where the hunt started. Conolly was supposed to have had a splendid horse. Still he was unable to get away from the man who kept following him. The fox was eventually caught and killed.

Conolly and his new friend were the only two who were there at the time and they were about to draw lots for the brush when the stranger agreed to give it to Conolly. Conolly invited his friend home to dinner. James Graham, the head groom, was ordered to take care of the stranger's horse.

After dinner the guests played a game of cards and the stranger was winning every game. A card fell on the floor. Conolly stooped down to pick it up and he noticed a cloven hoof instead of a foot on the strange man. Conolly called his servants and attendants and tried to get the stranger out of the house, but they failed. He sent his carriage for the RIC but they too were unable to get the stranger out of the house.

All the animals in the outhouses burst their doors and raced madly through the yards. Conolly sent for the Protestant minister of the place, but the stranger just laughed at him. He remained there for two days.

The gardener asked Conolly if he would go for the priest. Initially Conolly refused but at last he gave in and went himself for Father Kenny of Celbridge. When the priest arrived at the house he found the devil in a room burning up in a great fire.

The priest prayed for a long time and the devil disappeared through the hearth stone, leaving behind a large split in this stone.

The priest, Father Kenny, only lived for nine months afterwards.

THE DEVIL AND TOM CONOLLY

I found this little masterpiece of 'folk-art' in the 1911 edition of the Kildare Archaeological Society Journal, *p. 415, under the chapter entitled 'Ballads and Poems of the County Kildare'. The piece is entitled 'The Devil and Tom Conolly: An Eighteenth Century Legend of Castletown'. The author goes under the strange title of 'A Broth of a Boy (Russell)'.*

The ballad is based on Tom 'Squire' Conolly's encounter with the Black Earl of Hell. The terminology and turn of phrase is unique to the period and there is a good balance of humour and horror alike. The poor fox is referred to as 'Reynard' (an old folkloric name for the red fox or trickster) and the Devil as 'Auld Nick', giving the piece a sense of familiarity and empathy with the characters. You will notice that certain words are missing; this was common at the period so as to not cause offence or controversy to the family this ballad is based on. The Ballad first appeared in 1843 in The Dublin University Magazine, *Vol. xxii, p. 677 and was reprinted among 'The Kishoge Papers' in 1877.*

It is a brilliant piece of work that conjures up so much wonderful imagery and excitement, creating the archetypal great fireside tale.

'A southerly wind and a cloudy sky.
What a beautiful day for the Scent to lie!'
Says a huntsman old, with a very keen eye,
And a very red nose, to a whipper in by,
As he sits on the back of a very spruce hack,
And looks with delight on a beautiful pack
Of foxhounds as ever yet ran a track.

There were Howler and Jowler and Towser and Yelper
And boxer and pincher and Snarler and Skelper.
But Alas! And Alack! That it rests to be said,
That the last of the pack is some eighty years dead!
And the huntsman that sat on the back of the hack,
Died very soon after the last of the pack,
Having kept up the chase by good humour and mirth'
'Till Death one fine afternoon ran him to earth.

Rest to his bones! He has gone for aye,
And the sod lies cold on his colder clay;
He lists no more to the deep-mouthed bay,
Nor wakes the hills with his 'Hark Away!'
But never did a man with a hunting-whip rack
That I'd back at a fence against red-nosed Jack.

The cover is reached, and a better array
Of sportsmen it never has seen than to-day.
'Tis as gallant as all Ireland could yield:
The horsemen to all kinds of devilment steeled,
The best of the senate, the bench and the bar,
Whose mirth even Petty and Coke couldn't mar.

Bright spirits! Regarded with pride by a race
That loved Genius unmasked by Stupidity's face;
Nor fancied that Wisdom high places should quit
If she flung round her shoulders the mantle of wit!
The hunting-cap triumphs today o're the wig,
The ermine is doffed for a sportsmanlike rig;
But enough of the horsemen: the nags that they ride

Are as noble as horsemen might ever bestride;
In bottom or speed, few could match them indeed,
And if put to the pound wall of Ballinasloe,
There are plenty amongst them, who would never look,
'No!'

But the best mounted man at that gay coer-side
Is honest Tom Conolly, Castletown'a pride;
And mirth and good fellowship beam in his eye,
Such a goodly collection of guests to descry;
For guests shall be all, in Tom Conolly's hall,
Who keeps 'open house' for the great and the small;
And none who takes share in the fox-hunt today
Ere midnight from Castletown's mansion shall stray.

Right warm are the greetings that welcome the squire,
As he rides up-but the entire preamble will tire;
Besides that the hounds through the brushwood are dodging,
And making inquiries where Reynard is lodging;
Some snuffing the ground, with a caution profound;
Some running and poking their noses all round;
And now of the whole not a vestige is there,
But a number of tails cocked up in the air;
And now there's a bark, and a yelp, and a cry,
And the horsemen are still standing anxiously by;
And some of the pack
Are at length on the track;
And now there's a shout!
Sly old Reynard leaps out.

'Hold hard! Don't ride over the dogs!'
What a scramble!
Away go the hounds in the wake of the fox!
Away go the horsemen thro' brushwood and bramble!
Away go they all, o'er brooks, fences and rocks!
Afar in the plain, they are stretching amain:
Each sinew and nerve do the gallant steeds strain,
While the musical cry of the fleet footed hound
Is ringing in chorus melodiously round,
And the horseman who rides at the tail of the pack
Is a very tall gentleman, dressed all in black!

Away! Away! On his restless bed
His wearied limbs let the sluggard spread,
His eyes on the glorious morning close,
And fancy ease in that dull repose!
Give me to taste of the refreshing draught
Of the early breeze, on the green hill quaffed!
Give me to fly, with the lightning's speed
On the bounding back of the gallant steed!
Give me to bend o'er the floating mane,
While the blood leaps wild in each thrilling vein!
Oh! Who that has felt the joy intense,
To tempt the torrent, to dare the fence,
But feels each pleasure beside give place
To the manly danger that waits the chase?

Onward still – 'tis a spanking run
As e'er was seen by morning's sun!
Onward still, O'er plain the hill

Gad, 'tis a pace the Devil to kill!
A few of the nags it will puzzle, I trow,
To ride at that neat bit of masonry now.
Steady there, black fellow! – over he goes;
Well done, old bay! – ho! The brown fellow toes,
And pitches his rider clean out on his nose!
Eighteen out of fifty their mettle attest,
There's a very nice view from the road for the rest.

And now the 'boreen', with that rascally screen
Of furze on each bank – by old Nim, that's a poser!
There's the black fellow at it – 'Gad, over he goes, sir!'
Well done, Conolly! Stick to the brute, you dog!
Though he does seem old Beelzebub riding incog.
Ha! The third fellow's blown – No go, doctor, you're thrown,
And have fractured your 'Dexter Clavicular' bone;
Gad, here's the Solicitor-General down on him:
Who could think that he ever had got wig or gown on him?
Cleared gallantly! But sure, 'tis plain common sense,
Bar practice should fit a man well for a fence.
Five more show they're good ones, in bottom and speed;
But that tall, strange, black gentleman still keeps the lead!

Ha! Reynard, you're done for, my boy! At your back
Old Jowler and Clinker come, leading the pack;
Ay, close at your brush, they are making a rush;
Come face 'em old fellow, and die like a thrush!
Well snapped, but won't do, my poor 'modereen rue!'
That squeeze in the gullet has finished your breath;
And that very black horseman is in at the death!

The very black horseman dismounts from his steed
And takes off Reynard's brush with all sportsman-like heed;
Then patting the nag, with air of a wag,
Says, 'This is cool work, my old fellow, to-day!'
At which the black steed gives a very loud neigh;
And it is odd indeed, neither rider nor steed
Seems one whit the worse of their very great speed;
Though the next four or five, who this moment arrive,
Their horses all foaming, themselves all bemired,
Look beyond any doubt all heartily tired,
As they think, 'Who the deuce can be this chap in black,
Who has ridden all day at the tail of the pack?'

The group has come up with the stranger the while,
Who takes off his hat to the squire, with a smile,
And hands him the brush, with an air most polite,
Expressing his joy at transferring the right,
Which only the speed of the hunter had won
To him who had shown them so noble a run
And whose name, he would add, he had heard from a lad,
As a toast through all Ireland for humour and fun.

'Gad, sir,' says the squire,
'Whether most to admire, your politeness or daring I'm puzzled to say;
But though I've seen hunting enough in my day,
All I've met with must yield, to your feats in the field.
I trust I at least can induce you to dine,
And your horsemanship pledge in a bumper of wine;
And if longer you'll honour my house as a dweller.
All I promise you is you'll find more in the cellar.'

'Thanks Tom! I beg pardon, I make so d____d free,
When a man of your thorough good nature I see!
But excuse it'.
'Excuse it my excellent friend!
'Tis the thing of all others I wish you'd not mend;
None but good fellow had ever the trick.
But your name by the way?'
'Mine? Oh, pray call me Nick.'

'Very good, there's a spice of the devil about it!'
'A spice of the devil! Ay, faith, who can doubt it?
I'm dressed by the way in his livery sainted;
But they say the old boy's not as black as he's painted;
And this clerical suit ___'
'You're no parson sure come?'
'Ah, no pumping on that, my friend, Conolly ___mum!
This clerical suit, faith, though sombre and sad,
Is no bad thing at all, with the women, my lad!'

'Well done, Nick, on my life, I'll look after my wife,
If you came in way.'
'Gad,' says Nick with a laugh.
'To look after yourself, would be better by half'.
'Look after myself!' says the squire
'Lord! Why so? You've no partnership, sure, your namesake below?'
'No,' says Nick with a squint, 'I mean only to hint;
But I'll do it more plainly, for fear of mistake,
If we play at blind-hookey, be d____d wide awake'.
Then with laughter and jest, Honest Tom and his guest
Ride along, while their humour is shared by the rest,

Who vow, one and all, Master Nick to install,
As the prince of good fellows; and just at nightfall
They reach most good-humour'dly Castletown Hall.

'Tis a glorious thing when the wintry sun,
Ashamed of himself, has cut and run;
When the drizzling rain falls thick and fast,
And the shivering poplars stand aghast;
No sight abroad, but landscape bleak,
No sound, save whistle, and howl, and creak;
'Tis a glorious thing, in the dismal hour,
To be snugly housed from the tempest's power,
With a blazing fire, and a smoking board,
With all the best things of the season stored!
Not costly, mind, but good plain dinner,
To suit the wants of an erring sinner.

But enough, to their dinner the hunting folk sit!
With silence displaying more wisdom than wit.
But with dessert, wit begins to assert
His claims to attention; and near to its close
Takes the field while old wisdom goes off in a doze.

Then after a couple of bumpers of wine,
Ye gods, how the urchin commences to shine!
While, as for the stranger, his feats in the field
To his feats at the table unspeakably yield;
In drinking, in laughter, in frolic and jest,
He seems but the sun who gives light to the rest;

And after a while, when the squire begs a song from him,
He sings for them this, which grave folk will think wrong of him:

A fig for philosophy's rules!
Our stay is too brief upon earth,
To spare any time in the schools,
Save those of Love, Music and Mirth:
Yes! Theirs is exquisite lore
We can learn in life's summer by heart;
While the winter of gloomy four score
Leaves fools in philosophy's art.
Oh! Surely, if life's but a day,
'Tis vain o'er dull volumes to pine;
Let the sage choose what studies he may,
But Mirth, Love and Music be mine!

What a fool was Chaldea's old seer
Who studied the planters afar!
While the bright eye of woman is near;
My book be that beautiful star!
The lore of the planets who seeks
Is years in acquiring the art;
While the language dear woman's eye speaks
Is learned in a minute by her!
Then surely if life's but a day,
'Tis vain o'er dull volumes to pine;
Let the stars be his book as they may,
But the bright eye of woman be mine.

The chymist may learnedly tell
Of the treasures his art can unmask;
But the grape-juice has in it a spell
Which, is all of his lore that I ask.
In gazing on Woman's bright eyes
I feel all the star-student's bliss;
And chemistry's happiest prize
I find in a goblet like this!
Then fill up, if life's but a day,
What fool o'er dull volumes would pine?
Love and Mirth we can learn on the way,
And to praise them in music be mine!

'Hip, hip, hurrah!'
How they're cheering away.
'Hip, hip' They're growing uncommonly gay,
'Hip 'tis a way we've got in the' 'Hic-hiccup'
Lord! What a deuce of a shindy they kick up!
But at length they have done,
And drop off, one by one,
From their chairs, overcome by the claret and fun:
And at a quarter to four
All lie stretched out on the floor,
Enjoying in chorus a mighty fine snore;
While still to the claret, like gay fellows, stick
The warm-hearted squire and his jolly friend Nick!

There's a cooper of wine by Tom Conolly's chair
And he stoops for a bottle
At what does he stare?
My fine lad, you're found out!

There's the cloven foot plainly as the eye can behold.
'Cut your stick master Nick, if I may make so bold!
'Pon my life, what a jest, to have you as a guest.
You toping by dozens Lafitte's very best!
Be off sir, you've drunk of my wine to satiety.'

'No thank you,' says Nick; 'Tom I like your society,
I like your good humour. I relish your wit,
And I'm d____d but I very much like your Lafitte.
You may guess that your wine, has more bouquet than mine
And I'll stay, my old boy, in your mansion a dweller,
While a drop of such claret remains in your cellar!
I've my reasons for this, but 'twere needless to state 'em,
For this, my dear fellow, is my ultimatum!'

Tom rings for the flunkies: They enter, 'What now?'
He looks at Old Nick, with a very dark brow
And says, while the latter complacently bears
His glance 'Kick that insolent rascal downstairs!'
At their master's behest, they approach to the guest,
Though to kick him downstairs seems no joke at the best;
But when they draw near, with humours leer
Nick cries 'My good friends, you had better be civil.
'Tis not pleasant, believe me, to deal with the Devil!
I'm that much-abused person so do keep aloof,
And, lest you should doubt me, pray look at my hoof'.
Then lifting his leg in the air most polite,
He places the cloven hoof full in their sight,
When at once, with a roar, they all rush to the door;
And stumbling o'er wine-coopers, sleepers and chairs,
Never stop till they've got to the foot of the stairs.

The parson is sent for, he comes, 'tis no go,

Nick plainly defies him to send him below:

With a comical phiz, says he'll stay where he is,

And bids him be gone, for an arrant old quiz!

Asks how is his mother, and treats him indeed

With impertinence nothing on earth could exceed.

A pleasant finale, in truth, to a feast,

There's but one hope remaining, to send for a priest;

Though the parson on hearing it, says 'tis all fudge,

And vows that he never induce Nick to budge.

Still, as 'tis the sole hope of getting a severance

From Nick. The squire sends off at once for his reverence,

And would send for the Pope, if he saw any hope

That his power could induce the old boy to elope.

Father Malachy, sure that for Nick he's a match,

Doesn't ask better sport than to come to the scratch;

And arrives at the hall, in the midst of them all

While the frightened domestics' scarce venture to crawl:

And learning the state of affairs from the squire,

Says he'll soon make his guest from the parlour retire,

If he'll only agree, to give him rent free

A plot for a chapel; but if he refuses,

Master Nick may stay with him as long as he chooses.

'A plot for a chapel!' Tom Conolly cries

'Faith, I'll build one myself that will gladden your eyes,

If Old Nick cuts his stick.'

'That he shall double quick, if you undertake to stand
mortar and brick.'

'Agreed!' says the Squire; so the priest takes his book,
Giving Nick at the same time a terrible look
Then th' Exorcism begins, but Old Nick only grins,
And asks him to read out the 'Table of Sins';
'For between you and me, Holy Father' says he
'That's light and agreeable reading, you see,
And if you look it carefully over, I bet,
Your reverence will find you're a bit in my debt!'

At an insult so dire, Father Malachy's ire
Was aroused in an instant; so, closing the book,
He gives the arch-rascal one desperate look,
Then, with blessed precision, the volume lets fly,
And hits the arch-enemy fair in the eye!
There's a terrible yell that might startle all hell!
A flash, and a very strong brimstony smell!
And, save a great cleft, from his exit so deft
Not a trace of the gentleman's visit is left;
But the book, which was flung, in his visage was clung
To the wainscot, and sticks so tenaciously to it,
You'd fancy some means supernatural glue it;
And his reverence in fact finds it fixed to the mortar,
To the wonder of all, a full inch and a quarter!
Where the mark of it still to this day may be seen,
Or if not, they can show you where once it has been;

And if after that any doubts on it seize you,
All I can say is 'tis not easy to please you.

The delight of the Squire I, of course, can't express.
That 'tis boundless indeed you might easily guess
The very next day, he gives orders to lay,
The chapel's foundation; and early in May,
If in his excursions Nick happened to pass there;
And it stands to this day, slate, stone, mortar and brick
By Tom Conolly built, to get rid of Old Nick.

Since the period that Nick got this touch in the eye,
Of displaying his hoof he has grown very shy;
You can scarce find him out by his ill-shapen stump,
For he sticks to the rule: 'Keep your toe in your Pump!'

7

THE KILDARE
LURIKEEN

This is a lovely little story, taken from Patrick Kennedy's book
Fictions of the Celts, *published in 1866.*

A young girl who lived in sight of Castle Carbury, near
Edenderry, was going to the well for a pitcher of water one
summer morning, when who should she see sitting in a shel-
tered nook under an old thorn bush, but a Lurikeen, working
like vengeance at a little old brogue only fit for the foot of a
fairy like himself. There he was, boring his holes and jerking
his waxed ends, with his little three-cornered hat with gold
lace, his knee-breeches, his jug of beer by his side, and his
pipe in his mouth. He was so busy at his work, and so taken
up with an old ballad he was singing in Irish, that he did not
mind Breedheen till she had him by the scruff o' the neck.

'Ah, what are you doing?' says he, turning his head round as
well as he could. 'Dear, dear! To think of such a purty colleen
ketchin' a body, as if he was after robbin' a hen roost! What
did I do to be treated in such an un-decent manner? The very
vulgarest young ruffian in the townland could do no worse.
Come, come, Miss Bridget, take your hands off, sit down,
and let us have a chat, like two respectable people.'

'Ah, Mr Lurikeen, I don't care a wisp of borrach for your politeness. It's your money I want, and I won't take hand or eye from you till you put me in possession of a fine lob of it.'

'Money, indeed! Ah! Where would a poor cobbler like me get it? There's no money hereabouts, and if you'll only let go my arms, I'll turn my pockets inside out, and open the drawer of my seat, and give you leave to keep every halfpenny you'll find.'

'That won't do. My eyes will keep going through you like darning needles till I have the gold,' she said. 'Begonies, if you don't make haste, I'll carry you, head and pluck, into the village, and there you'll have thirty pair of eyes on you instead of one.'

'Well, well! Was ever a poor cobbler so circumvented! And if it was an ignorant, ugly bosthoon that done it, I would not wonder; but a decent, comely girl, that can read her *Poor Man's Manual* at the chapel, and ...'

'You may throw your compliments on the stream there' they won't do for me, I tell you,' said Breedheen. 'The gold, the gold, the gold! Don't take up my time with your blarney.'

'Well, if there's any to be got, its undher the auld castle it is; we must have a walk for it. Just put me down, and we'll get on,' he said.

'Put you down indeed! I know a trick worth two of that; I'll carry you.'

'Well, how suspicious we are! Do you see the castle from this?' Bridget was about turning her eyes from the little man to where she know the castle stood, but she bethought herself in time.

They went up a little hillside, and the Lurikeen was quite reconciled, and laughed and joked; but just as they got to the brow, he looked up over the ditch, gave a great screech, and shouted just as if a bugle horn was blew at her ears. 'Oh, murdher! Castle Carbury is afire.' Poor Biddy gave a great

start, and looked up towards the castle. The same moment she missed the weight of the Lurikeen, and she let go of him and when her eyes fell where he was a moment before, there was no more sign of him than if everything that passed was a dream.

Not long after that in Kildare a boy caught himself a leprechaun and demanded that it told him where money was hidden. The leprechaun stuck a stick in the ground and told the boy to get a spade and dig in that exact spot, there, he said was where the money would be found. However, when the boy returned with a spade he found hundreds of sticks stuck all over the field. He had been tricked. For it is a well-known fact that you must never turn your back on a wee leprechaun when you are lucky enough to catch one, for they are notorious tricksters and rogues.

8

THE GUBBAWN SEER

There are many stories collected about this character and his adventures. Some were collected by Patrick Kennedy in 1866 and by Ella Young in 1927. They span the length and breadth of Ireland. I came across this one by Ms Greene of Milbrook, which is specifically based in Kildare. The Gubbawn Seer was a highly skilled smith, architect and carpenter who lived during the seventh century. But he was most famous for his wit and sharp senses and how that rubbed off on others, depending on if their hearts were in the right place. Gubbawn Seer means Gubbawn the Builder. He was also known as the Wondersmith.

The Gubbawn Seer was a carpenter. He was a first rate tradesman at all things. One day, he gave his son a sheep-skin, and told him he wouldn't let him get married until he brought back the skin and the price of it. So the son used to carry the sheepskin under his arm to Athy every Tuesday; but he could never get anyone to give him the skin and the price of it. There was a girl who lived at Barker's Ford, Inch River, and he used to see her when he was passing by. One day she said to him, 'Musha, what do you be carryin' that sheepskin every Tuesday to Athy for?' So he told her the reason. She took the skin off him, went in and plucked the wool off it; then she brought it out and the money for the wool in her hand: 'Here now,' says she, 'here's the skin and the price of it.' The Gubbawn was so impressed he told his son to marry that girl.

After the marriage the Gubbawn and his son were going somewhere to work, quite far away, and the Gubbawn said to his son; 'Come, shorten the road.' The son said he couldn't, so the Gubbawn said the two of them should return home.

So the two started back again. When the son's wife saw them back again, she said, 'Why, I thought you were at your journey's end by now,' and the son said, 'My father bid me to shorten the road, and I couldn't, so then he made us return.' The wife told him, when they started again tomorrow morning, and when they got to the same place, that the Gubbawn ask him to shorten the road again. When this happened the son was to start a jig or a verse of a song. And so he did; and the Gubbawn Seer said, 'That's right now, come on, I see you know how to do it.' That's how the son shortened the road.

There was another story in which a king sent for the Gubbawn and his son to create a magnificent building in England – one the likes never seen before. The king had planned when it was built to put the two to death, so they could not build anything more beautiful elsewhere.

The Gubbawn heard of this plot somehow. When the king asked him was the building finished, the Gubbawn replied that it was not. He told him he needed a special tool that he had left at home and that he would have to get it himself.

Instead, the king sent the Gubbawn's son and his own son, the prince, to get it. The tool was supposed to be in a great big old chest and the son's wife asked the prince to find it. The minute the prince put his arm in, she took him by the heels and heaved him down into it. She sent back a message to the king, saying she would cut his head off if he did not send back her father-in-law. So the king had to send back the Gubbawn Seer.

Another story about the Gubbawn Seer tells of how he heard that the King of Lies, who lived in Dublin, was looking for someone to tell a better lie than he ever could. The king loved tall tales and was such a good liar he was sure no one would be able to beat him. Anyone who managed would be given great wealth. Many people took up the king's challenge and all failed. As punishment for their failure, the king cut off their heads. The Gubbawn, however, was confident that he would triumph so he left Kildare and headed off to Dublin to see the king. When he arrived at the castle he saw all the heads of those who had failed the test on spikes outside the palace.

The king was there to meet him with all his servants and soldiers watching with great enthusiasm. Two of the soldiers grabbed the Gubbawn so that he might not flee and the king began boasting about the chickens he had, how they were as big as horses and how he ate three cows and two sheep a day, washed down by seven kegs of whiskey. The Gubbawn Seer replied with all sorts of tall tales and fanciful stories, but the king was not impressed and he was about to lift his axe and cut off the Gubbawn's head.

Then the Gubbawn calmly began telling the king about his journey to Dublin from Kildare and how he had met an ass along the way that was looking very sad. He asked the ass why he was so full of sorrow and the ass replied that he was once a king and the fairies had put a spell on him. The Gubbawn Seer asked him why and he replied that he was too proud and full of himself so they turned him into

an ass and turned an ass into a king. 'What king would that be now?' asked the Gubbawn and the ass replied, 'The one that you are on your way to see in Dublin, for he truly is an ass'.

The king was furious when he heard this and shouted at the top of his voice at the Gubbawn Seer 'You're a liar!' With that the king had no choice but to tell the soldiers to release him. He put down his axe and handed over a bag of gold and jewels to the Gubbawn, who thanked the king politely and made his way home to Kildare.

9

THE BOG OF ALLEN

The Bog of Allen is a vast plain of peatland in the centre of Ireland, covering over 370 square miles. Its borders touch the counties of Offaly, Meath, Laois, Westmeath and, of course, Kildare. There is a sense of foreboding about the place and it houses many secrets and stories, one of which is that of Poll the Pishogue, the Kildare witch. The bog is millions of years old and within its dark depths, prehistoric walkways were found, suggesting that pre-historic man lived there and who knows what other creatures before that. I found this story in a great little book called Irish Ghosts *by J. Aeneas Corcoran, published by Geddes & Grosset in 2002.*

In the dreary, featureless flats of the Bog of Allen, especially in the days before much of it was drained, reclaimed for cultivation and for the harvesting of turf. Vague, indistinct shapes could sometimes be seen by travellers, only a little darker than the grey sky itself, lingering among the peaty pools and black sumps of the surface. From a distance they looked like human figures, and were thought to lure unsuspecting wayfarers into the treacherous depths of the bog. There were areas of soft mud, of unknown depth, where these unfortunates would be swallowed up and would die a hideous, choking death as the slime engulfed them.

One traveller recorded an experience that might confirm this impression. Walking in the Bog of Allen, on a well-known path, he was overtaken by a heavy rainstorm. The sky was so darkened by clouds that he feared he would lose the path. Then in the distance he saw a low cabin, an indistinct shape in the rain. Hoping for shelter from the downpour, he made his way towards it. As he came nearer, he saw it was a derelict house, long abandoned, with no glass in any of its windows, and the roof half-collapsed. Nevertheless, it offered some respite and so he went in.

Standing in the doorway, eating his rain-soaked sandwiches, he looked out, hoping to see the sky brighten up. Not far away, the dark loops of a stream wound their way across the bogland. At one point on the stream's bank he saw what appeared to be a dark patch of haze, like fog, and yet not fog. Knowing that the bogland had strange atmospherics of its own, he was not unduly puzzled, and yet it gave him a somewhat eerie feeling. This feeling was greatly intensified when he saw that the hazy patch was moving over the surface of the bog in his direction. There was a sense of purpose in that steady movement that made him feel something was directing its course straight at him; something that was not friendly to humanity. As happens in a nightmare, he felt himself unable to move from the doorway as the darkness loomed up, blotting out everything else in the landscape.

As it reached him, his terror reached a climax. It was completely dark, and he seemed to feel arms brushing past him. He was convinced that something terrible was about to happen to him. But then, suddenly, it was gone. It had

moved on, through the ruined house and onward into the expanse of bogland beyond.

Gulping and gasping for breath, he staggered round the corner of the house, oblivious of the still pouring rain, to see it dwindle and vanish into the distance. Whatever it was, some cold, lonely, shapeless spirit of the marsh, it had no more concern for him than if it had been the wind. But the terror that it induced was very far from natural. The traveller never returned to the Bog of Allen again and was always wary of travelling in remote areas after dark.

For anyone now planning on visiting this ancient vast plain be wary of what might be lurking in the shadowy depths of the Bog of Allen.

10

THE GHOST ROOM AT MAYNOOTH

I found this story in a great little book called Irish Ghosts *by J. Aeneas Corcoran published by Geddes & Grosset 2002.*

In his book, *Window on Maynooth*, Father Denis Meehan mentions the existence of a haunted room at Maynooth College. One of the main blocks of the complex of buildings is called Rhetoric House and this is what he has to say about it:

> The most interesting feature of Rhetoric House will certainly be the ghost room. The two upper floors are altogether residential, and the ghost room is, or rather was, Room 2, on the top corridor. It is now an oratory of St Joseph. Legend, of course, is rife concerning the history of this room, but unfortunately everything happened so long ago that no one can now guarantee anything like accuracy. The incident, whatever it may have been, is at least dated to some extent by a Trustees' resolution of 23 October 1860: 'That the President be authorised to convert Room 2 of the top corridor of Rhetoric House into an Oratory of St Joseph, and to fit up an Oratory of St Aloysius in the prayer hall of the Junior Students.'

The story, as it is commonly now detailed for the edification of susceptible freshmen, begins with a suicide. The student resident in this room killed himself one night. According to some he used a razor, but tellers of the story are not too careful about such details. The next inhabitant, it is alleged, felt irresistibly compelled to follow suit, and again, according to some, he did. A third, or it may have been the second, to avoid a similar impulse, and when actually about to use his razor, jumped through the window into Rhetoric Yard. He broke some bones, but his life was spared.

Subsequently no student could be induced to use the room but a priest volunteered to sleep or keep vigil there for one night. In the morning, his hair was white, though no one dares to relate what his harrowing experiences might have been. Afterwards the front wall of the room was removed and a small altar of Saint Joseph was erected.

The basic details of the story have doubtless some foundation in fact, and it is safe to assume that something very unpleasant did occur. The suicide (or suicides), in so far as one can deduce from the oral tradition that remains, seem to have taken place in the period 1842–48. A few colourful adjuncts that used to form part of the stock-in-trade of the storyteller are passing out of memory now. Modern students for instance do not point out the footprint burned in the wood, or the blood marks on the walls. This is wise, for who knows what they may invite into their midst. But some say that they have seen strange shapes accompanied by low, baleful sounds at night in the area where the ghost room used to be.

11

THE GHOST AT CLONGOWES

This story is taken from the Kildare Archaeological Society Journal Vol. III *and describes a chilling tale from Clongowes Wood College, a secondary school for boys. Clongowes has a great history. James Joyce attended there and it has the most magnificent grounds and sports facilities, including one of the best nine-hole golf courses in Ireland.*

While Marshal Brain, serving in the Austrian service, was fighting abroad, his two sisters lived at Clongowes. Tragedy struck when he was killed at the Battle of Prague in 1757.

Meanwhile, back at the mansion, the servants were all seated around the fire in the ironing room. Suddenly, the door to the room was wide open and so was the hall door. The servants were astonished to see an army officer in a white uniform enter the hall and go up the stairs. He seemed to glide there, as there was no sound of footsteps or even a creaking of stairs. His hands were pressed to this breast, from which blood was flowing down his white uniform.

He then burst into a flaming pariah with a terrible scream and disappeared without a trace. When they recovered from

the shock of this sight, they rushed up the stairs to inform the sisters.

The sisters had seen nothing unusual, but on hearing a full description, realised that it had been their brother, and that he must have met his death on the battlefield.

Masses were immediately celebrated for him, and a wake was held. Two weeks later a dispatch came announcing the Marshal's death, the very date and time the apparition was seen walking up the stairs.

Some people believed that the servants might have made up this story, so that they might profit from the wake celebrations. But, it could not be explained how ordinary working people from County Kildare, who had never left the country, described in detail and with conviction an Austrian Marshal's uniform.

12

THE HUNGRY HALL

This story was collected by Seamus Cullen as part of the schools collection that was conducted between 1937 and 1938 for the Irish Folklore Commission. It was part of a number of folklore stories written by Mary Gill and Nan Crowe, two sixth-class pupils from St Mochuo National School in Rathcoffey. This was the school I attended myself as a child. I only found this story recently and maybe it is a good thing, for sometimes ignorance is bliss, especially when you live out in the middle of the countryside and the nights are pitch black and the air is full of baleful sounds and chilling winds.

Hungry Hall is an old placename in the townland of Barreen. It is situated approximately 160 yards south of Balraheen crossroads and one mile north of Rathcoffey. The name refers to a gateway that leads into a division of land and its origin comes from a very dark story that took place in the early nineteenth century.

It all began when young boys from the area started disappearing in the general Rathcoffey area. Despite exhaustive search parties and thorough investigations, no trace of the missing children was found.

One day, a man travelling in the Balraheen area close to Rathcoffey was passing by a house and needed to light his clay pipe. The house was a thatched house and had a half-door and an old woman and her son lived there. The traveller was in the habit of getting a light for his pipe from the woman in the house. However, on this occasion the woman was not in the house and, despite calling out her name, he got no reply.

As the door was open, he decided to enter the house and help himself to a light. There was a big cooking pot over the fire and the traveller bent down to the fire to get a cinder in order to light his pipe. As he bent down he saw the foot of a child sticking out from the pot. The poor man got such a shock that he immediately ran out from the house screaming. He went and told another man who was walking along the road. The proper authorities were called and an investigation took place.

The woman of the house was arrested and eventually brought before the local magistrate, Thomas Wogan Browne, from Castlebrown. Wogan Browne served two terms as a magistrate, firstly, for some years before 1797 and secondly, for a four-year period between 1806 and 1810 so the incident must have happened within one of those periods. At her trial she was accused of cannibalism and she admitted the charge. The woman seemed unfazed by the whole thing and went on to give a full statement on the events.

Seemingly she lured the children into her house by offering them food. The judge, who was also a landlord in the area, informed her that he had many fine bullocks on his property and wondered why she didn't take any of his cattle. She smiled at him in a way that would turn your blood to ice and replied,

'Your Lordship, if only you tasted the flesh of young boys (which she described as tastier than veal), you would never eat another scrap of animal meat.' This remark horrified the court and not surprisingly she was sentenced to death.

Executions at the period would usually take place at the scene of the crime. Many highwaymen, also known as rapparees or tories, who were caught and convicted of robbery in the eighteenth and nineteenth centuries were taken back to the scene of their crime and hanged there.

The execution of this woman took place close to her house at Barreen. There was a large tree beside the house and a rope was placed across a branch of the tree and there she was hanged. The issue of how best to dispose of her remains had already been discussed. As one convicted of eating human flesh, she would not be allowed to be buried in consecrated ground. Therefore during the hanging a barrel of tar was placed under her body and the tar set on fire. When her body fell into the barrel it was consumed in the flames. She was regarded in the local area as a witch and her execution is the last recorded burning of a witch in the locality. This suggests that there were other witch burnings before her in the area, but no details survive.

The house where she lived was never again occupied and soon became a ruin. Due to the incident, both the house and the adjoining division of land came to be known as Hungry Hall.

The story of the horrific events at Hungry Hall was often told to children in order to get them to go to bed early and that is one of the reasons why the story survived in folklore to modern times.

In later years a black dog, thought to be the witch in disguise, was often seen running from Hungry Hall to the crossroads nearby.

There is also speculation that her ghost roams the area. Dressed in white robes, she goes by the name of the White Lady. She has been seen wandering the roads and walking alongside weary, frightened travellers. She sings a haunting lullaby, the same lullaby that she used to entice the children into her house of Macabre. So if you are in the area, be wary of a woman dressed in white. She may stop you for a lift and who knows what may happen.

13

THE WHITE LADY

This is a great ghost story that I got from a well-respected local historian Seamus Cullen. The story also appeared in Patrick Kennedy's Legendry Fictions of the Irish Celts *published 1866. I remember as a child hearing about the white lady and when I looked out my window on a windy night I thought of her as I watched the white sheets on the washing line fluttering and billowing like dancing ghosts.*

According to Seamus this story took place around 1860, during which time farm produce was brought to Dublin by horse and cart. This included food and bedding for Dublin's many dairy cows, which was delivered from places like Rathcoffey and Clane.

Pat Gill lived about two miles north of Rathcoffey and was one of the major transporters of hay and straw to Dublin. The route he took was a road taken by many from the Donadea–Rathcoffey area by way of the Baltracey crossroads to Lady Chapel and on to Celbridge. This road has not changed so much until you come to the outskirts of Maynooth and then it's motorway all the way. Anyway, one evening the bold Pat was on his way to Dublin city with his cart piled high with hay and straw for the dairy and he headed for the Lady Chapel crossroads. The junction is still there today but a whole lot busier. Pat decided to do something that would be highly illegal and dangerous now, but back then it was fine. He decided to have a little sleep while he was driving. The auld horse was well used to taking this journey on a regular basis and it knew the way. I suppose it was like an early form of auto-pilot.

As Pat was passing Baltracey Mill, which is situated half a mile from the crossroads, he was having a grand wee snooze and popping an eye open every once in a while to check his horse. Then, all of a sudden, poor auld Pat got the fright of his life when saw a woman dressed in long white clothes appear out of nowhere and start crossing the road. She came up to the horse and walked on with him, close by his neck. Pat pulled the reins on the horse's head to the opposite side of the figure, for fear the animal should tread on her feet or long robes, but she did not move away and calmly walked on alongside the horse. Pat was sure that at one point he could see right through her robes and there was nobody to be seen, only the other side of the road.

Poor Pat was scared now but he could not keep his eyes off this strange silent creature that had appeared out of nowhere and insisted on walking alongside his horse. He was wondering what he should do. Should he stop or keep going? What if this creature was a malevolent spirit and became angry with him if he stopped? He was perplexed by the situation and terrified at the same time. The horse seemed happy enough and was not bothered by his new companion and just trotted along happily.

The centre of the crossroads at Barreen had a patch of green in the middle and traffic would pass on either side.

When Pat came to its edge, the white figure stood still, while the cart turned and it seemed as though a part of the shaft of the cart on one side passed straight through her, like she had been impaled.

When Pat saw this he got an awful fright and he cried out, 'By your leave ma'am!' but the white figure said nothing at all.

On shot the horse and cart and it flew on down the road. Pat was afraid to look back, for he was sure he had killed the woman. But his conscience had got the better of him and he stopped and looked back. And there he saw the white apparition standing in the centre of the plot of grass, her hand placed over her forehead to shade her eyes from the sun, as she looked solemnly after him. Pat never took his stare off the woman until he turned around the bend. Then he heard the sound of a low mournful cry fly above his head and a terrible chill passed through his body and there was a dreadful sadness in the air. Poor Pat carried on to Dublin, but he did not sleep for the rest of the journey, and he made sure to stay the night at an inn in the city, for he would not dare return home at night along the stretch of road where he had seen the white lady.

Who was this strange, shrouded figure and where did she come from? The spectre appeared close to a spot where some sixty years earlier a woman was executed for the monstrous crime of cannibalism. Some people say the figure is that of the mother of one of the poor boys, looking in vain for her lost son. But most believe that the spectre is that of the cannibal woman herself, maybe hunting for new victims to feed her diabolical appetite. The crossroads is only 150 metres from the site of the cannibalism transgression, known as the Hungry Hall.

Local people who live in and around the area where the story took place still say that they have seen strange sightings of a white figure haunting the roads at night. Indeed, many say that Kildare is the most haunted county in Ireland.

14

Nellie Clifden and the Curragh Wrens

I wish to thank Dr Mary Ellen Leighton for her help in putting together this powerful and moving story.

'The Curragh of Kildare', also known as 'The Winter it is Past'

The winter it is past and the summer's come at last.
The birds they are singing in the trees.
Their little hearts are glad, but mine is very sad
For my true love is far away from me
And straight I will repair to the Curragh of Kildare
For it's there I'll find tidings of my dear.

The rose upon the briar by the water running clear
Brings joy to the linnet and the deer.
Their little hearts are blessed, but mine knows no rest
For my true love is far away from me
And straight I will repair to the Curragh of Kildare
For it's there I'll find tidings of my dear.

A livery I will wear and I'll comb back my hair
And in velvet so green I will appear
And straight I will repair to the Curragh of Kildare
For it's there I'll find tidings of my dear
And straight I will repair to the Curragh of Kildare
For it's there I'll find tidings of my dear.

I'll wear a cap of black with some frills around my neck.
Golden rings on my fingers I will wear.
Oh yes, this I'll undertake for my own true lover's sake
For he lives in the Curragh of Kildare
And straight I will repair to the Curragh of Kildare
For it's there I'll find tidings of my dear.

Oh, you who are in love and cannot it remove
I pity the pain you do endure
For experience lets me know that your hearts are full of woe
'Tis a woe that no mortal can endure
And straight I will repair to the Curragh of Kildare
For it's there I'll find tidings of my dear.

An Irish folk song, mid-1700s

The song 'The Curragh of Kildare' is a beautiful and melancholic portrayal of a young woman who disguises herself to go and find her lover who has gone to the army camp at the Curragh in County Kildare. This woman would have been referred to at the time as a 'camp follower'. These were the wives, lovers and partners of the soldiers who followed their men as they travelled.

The best-known version of the text, usually referred to by the title The Winter it is Past, *is attributed to the Scottish poet*

Robert Burns. Burns appears to have developed it from an existing ballad, entitled The Lovesick Maid, which referred to a high-wayman called Johnson, who was hanged in 1750 for robbery in the Curragh of Kildare. Burns changed the original text considerably and removed two stanzas referring directly to Johnson. The resulting ballad was published in the collection The Scots Musical Museum, published between 1787 and 1803.

There have been different versions of the song recorded over the years and it has been popularised by several well-known artists. But the version above is the one that I grew up listening to. I often wondered how such a sad and haunting song came to pass and what happened to these women who went to the Curragh of Kildare.

Well, I was to find out and it was no wonder that this is a song that talks of love as an emotion that no mortal can endure. For the camp followers that were rejected by their men, left behind to fend for themselves when their men were posted overseas, or who fell pregnant out of wedlock were to face a fate worse than death and indeed a woe that no mortal can endure. They were to become 'wrens' because they lived in holes in the banks and covered themselves with furze bushes to protect themselves from the bitter and brutal weather conditions. They were given this name from an old song that was and still is sung traditionally by 'wren boys' on 'Wren Day' (Saint Stephen's Day or Boxing Day on 26 December).

The wren, wren, the king of all birds
On St Stephen's Day was caught in the Furze.

There have been songs, stories and plays written about the Curragh Wrens. Even Charles Dickens wrote of their terrible plight. Today they have their own dark folklore in and around Kildare. And this is their story.

The story of the Curragh Wrens first came to light when a journalist called James Greenwood from the London newspaper the *Pall Mall Gazette* (edited by Charles Dickens) heard mysterious little stories wafting over from the Curragh in Kildare to London. They were stories about a certain colony of poor wretches who lived in conditions that were subhuman and died like stray dogs in the London streets. In these stories there was always something so shocking that comfortable people were glad to disbelieve them and something so strange that it was easy to disregard them as fireside tales of terror. No one could believe that in a Christian, police-regulated society like their own that people could be expected to live in such conditions.

This seemed all the more unlikely because the Curragh was not an unfrequented nook in some distant corner of the land, but a plain near the capital city of Dublin. The Curragh Camp was an encampment wherein thousands of Englishmen as well as thousands of Irishmen constantly lived (both a gentle and simple life), and where scores of strangers, visitors, would go there for no other purpose but to see what was to be seen, peer about every week of every summer season. It did not seem at all natural that things so very unlike what ought to happen in the respectable and quaint Victorian nineteenth century could go on from year to year without investigation, arrest and scandal. So Charles Dickens thought it worth while to ask James Greenwood, 'a hardy man of brains' to go and look into the matter.

Dickens requested that Greenwood go to the camp, and find the wrens (if any), and visit their nests (if any), and spend time enough by day and night amongst them to let him know the nature of these peculiar people, about whom so many incredible hints had been given and forgotten. And this is what Greenwood reported back:

… it was on an evening before September had cooled – three weeks ago and more – that I set out to investigate the manners and customs, the habits and habitat, of a bird not unknown indeed in England, nor even in London, but reported to be on the Curragh of a seriously peculiar kind.

From London to Holyhead, from Holyhead to Kingstown [now known as Dun Laoghaire, County Dublin], from Kingstown to Dublin – all this was within the limits of civilization. Dublin – yes, Dublin is a civilized city: there is not courage enough in the world to deny it. To Kildare my steps were directed, for that town is nearer than any other to the Curragh camp: – thence could I most easily go a-nesting.

From Dublin to Kildare, passed much squalor and degradation, Greenwood described seeing wretched huts and hovels that seem to grow out of the earth like grotesque toadstools. And around them was a plethora of poverty and idleness, the likes of which he had never seen before.

In Kildare Greenwood found a man called Jimmy Lynch who agreed to drive him over to the camp. During the journey Jimmy regaled Greenword with stories about his mare, 'Scottish Queen', and the mighty boxer Dan Donnelly, whom he believed was the greatest fighter of all time.

Greenwood was only half-listening and looked away to the vast plains where an army lived all the year round. Breaking into Jimmy's raptures about the Scottish Queen, he asked him how many soldiers were on the camp. 'Well, thin, tin or twelve thousand, maybe and a mighty fine time they have of it,' replied Jimmy with a glint in his eye. Greenwood asked him if their wives or sweethearts were with them. Jimmy replied: 'Widout their wives, shure, and what of that, yer hanner? But some of their wives is with them, I believe, good luck to them! Though there's no sweethearts in the camp at all, divil a one!'

'But over there!' Pointing vaguely with his whip across the plains, Jimmy's jovial mood changed and a iciness came about the affair as he directed Greenwood's eye towards the outskirts of the camp. 'There's many of them poor devils living in places made of furze inthirely. Winther and summer, in a bit of a bush.'

'Wrens don't you call them?' said Greenwood, trying to catch a glimpse of his reporter's quarry.

'Wrins! That's the name ov 'em, Wrins! That's what they do call 'em, and a dridful life they lade. Most distrissing, believe me!' Jimmy's final remark was obviously something he had heard from others he had taken to the camp, describing what they saw.

There was a moment of silence and Jimmy sought relief again in the virtues of his mare, while Greenwood's eyes wandered over the plains where many a furze bush was visible, but none which looked as if it could be inhabited by any creatures but birds of the air and beasts of the field.

On the Curragh the air was strong; an easterly wind was blowing over its miles of wasteland – dead level for the most part, but with undulations here and there, and broken by mounds and raths, stretching along for a considerable distance and at a height at least distinguishable.

The turf was soft and elastic everywhere. Sheep browsed upon it and there you could see the Irish shepherd. Greenwood saw a beautiful shepherdess flustering her rags out of their natural repose in an attempt to separate the sheep marked this way from the sheep marked that. She wore no bonnet on her head, revealing abundant locks, and below her ragged skirts a pair of shapely legs.

The Scottish Queen ambled along. There were good roads from Kildare to the camp, and from time to time they met cars containing well-buttoned military men. Other military men were seen, in ones and twos and threes, lounging: moving patches of red amongst the dark-green masses of furze.

Jimmy had no precise instructions; he was to drive upon the Curragh, and that's all; but he had a notion that Greenwood wanted to go to the camp, and particularly to the Hollow, the actual spot where the boxer Cooper was beaten by the immortal Dan Donnelly. He had no idea that his passenger wanted to see something that no regular tourist would wish or need to see.

In this somewhat aimless way they came to a series of block huts, extending for approximately two miles, on either side of the road. Here and there a few groups of soldiers were seen lounging listlessly, or engaged in some athletic sport. Jimmy pointed out each object of interest as they drove along. 'And that's the Catholic chapel, your hanner. And that's the Prodestan' church. And this is Donnelly's Hollow' (strewn with many canvas tents) 'where the fight was! Hould the mare, sir! hould Scottish Queen, and, bedad! I'll show ye where Cooper stood, and where Donnelly stood – well I know the futmarks ov 'em!' Jimmy would not be denied this opportunity to show where his hero had once stood. And those footprints are still there to this day, but that's another story.

Fortunately, the Scottish Queen restrained the fiery impulses of her blood, and stood still like any carthorse while Jimmy planted himself in Donnelly's footmarks, and tried to satisfy the last object of Greenwood's journey by putting himself in a fighting attitude on that heroic spot. With as little shock to his feelings Greenwood made him aware that he didn't care too much about Cooper or Donnelly; that the afternoon was too far advanced for a regular visit to the camp itself, but that in driving back he should like to get a glimpse of the wrens' nests.

Jimmy put his hands down slowly, and in silence remounted the car. The soldiers he could understand as the object of a tourist's gaze, and Donnelly's Hollow as the object of his excitement. But 'Thim Wrins!' sighed poor Jimmy, exasperated.

However, back they went through the line of huts; the road dwindled, and they were presently driving over the plains. By this time the air was fast growing colder and mistier. The block huts of the camp could only be seen as a dim outline, soon they were the only hints of human life in the dreary prospect.

As far as the eye could distinguish within the waning limits of the light, all was barren and cheerless. The sky above looked waste as the plain itself, and drearier, for there were still those constantly recurring patches of furze to break the green monotony below, while there was nothing at all to break the grey monotony above.

How in such solitary places at such times the mind also seems to close in from above and on all sides in a twilight sort of way, like one has found oneself in a strange haunting dream. Greenwood soon found his mind in this condition as they rolled over the noiseless turf; so that it was with a start a presently saw a bare-headed, bare-footed woman standing only a few feet away. Had the figure sprung out of the earth or dropped from the clouds? His surprise could not have been greater; true though it was that he had come to Ireland to see this very woman and her companions. 'There's a wrin, sir!' Jimmy shouted at that moment, 'and there's a nest! And there's another!' But Greenwood saw no nest.

The clumps of furze looked a little thicker than usual in the direction indicated, but there was nothing more remarkable about them. But when, jumping from the car, Greenwood walked a few paces onward; he understood better now what nesting on the Curragh was. These heaps of furze were built and furnished for human occupation; and here and there outside them were squatted groups of those who dwelt therein. 'Winther and summer in a bit of a bush.' Not one or two, but several groups – half naked, destitute and wretched. There seemed to be a considerable colony.

Greenwood spent a long night amongst them afterwards. He found out all that was worth knowing of a tribe of outcasts as interesting, perhaps, as any which the scientific men of the Abyssinian expedition were likely to write books about.

Greenwood stated there were ten 'nests' in all, accommodating about sixty women aged between seventeen and twenty-five, some of whom had been there for up to nine years.

Each nest was individually numbered and consisted of a rough shelter measuring some nine feet by seven feet and about four and a half feet from the ground.

You had to crouch down and crawl inside as a beast would have to crouch for cover and there was no standing upright once you were inside. He described them as big, rude birds' nests, compacted with harsh branches and turned topsy-turvy on the ground. There was no chimney, not even a hole in the roof, which generally sloped forward. The smoke from the fire, which burned on the floor of the hut, had to pass through the door when the wind was right, otherwise it reeked slowly through the crannied walls. In some of these nests there were as many as eight women. In them they slept, cooked and ate. If they were sick, they would just lie there and there they would die.

The nests were in various levels of decay and disrepair. Greenwood was taken in by nest Number 5. Outside he saw a beautiful girl, neatly dressed in a clean, starched cotton gown, bright white cotton stockings and well-fitting boots. She was washed and her hair was combed. Squatting outside were two dishevelled-looking wretches, wearing filthy frieze petticoats, thrown loosely over their backs. Their hair was tangled and dirty and straggled over their naked shoulders and unwashed faces. One of the women was holding a small infant to her breast and was making very strong looks at Jimmy the car-man.

The pretty girl addressed, saying in perfectly good English, 'Good day Sir, and will you walk into our little house?' At the same moment the girl who was holding the child, squatting by the front of nest rose up and attacked Jimmy, using terrible language and obscenities. It seemed that Jimmy had known this girl previously and this matter proved to raise some questions.

Greenwood went inside the nest, leaving Jimmy to deal with the young woman who was determined to verbally attack him and rightly so if this was the predicament that he had left the poor girl and child in. Inside he saw a shelf to hold a teapot, crockery, a candle, and a box in which the women kept their few possessions. Upturned saucepans were used as stools, and the musty straw for bedding was pushed to one side during the day. At night the fire within the shelter was covered with a perforated pot, and the women undressed to sleep in the straw. In summertime the nests gave some shelter, but in winter the wind whistled through them.

When Greenwood crawled out of the nest, the attractive young girl said she hoped that he would come again when they were less occupied with domestic cares. She had introduced herself as Miss Clancy. Jimmy was still being attacked and when he saw he could now leave, he hopped up on the car without any hesitation and turned to Greenwood, exclaiming, 'Did anyone iver hear the like ov them divils? It's disgusting entirely!' Greenwood being a gentleman of principle and standing, realised it was a sceptical situation and did not indulge in any of Jimmy's fanciful talk and quickly ordered him to drive on.

Although Jimmy wanted to race the Scottish Queen out of the place, Greenwood insisted that he trot slowly through the camp so he could get a good look at what was going on around him and speak to the women there.

He found out that all the women were Irish and came from different parts of the country. They were seen as fallen women and outcasts of what was considered respectable society. Some of them had followed a soldier from another station, others came to seek a former lover, while the majority had come because of necessity or desperation. Some were women who became pregnant out of wedlock and followed their estranged lover to the camp and lost them there, or were admonished with blows and told to go away. Some in the same condition were banished by a lord or master who had his way with them and now saw them as an embarrassment and nuisance.

The women lived, received their families, gave birth and died in the 'nests'. Their clothing consisted of a frieze skirt with nothing on top except another frieze around the shoulders. In the evenings when the younger women went to meet the soldiers in the uninhabited gorse patches, they dressed up in crinolines, petticoats and shoes and stockings.

The older women remained behind to mind the children. Greenwood counted four older women altogether, and they also prepared food.

It must have been heartbreaking to see children and babies living in such conditions, but they seemed to be well looked after and were given priority when it came to milk and fresh nourishment. Greenwood stated that the babies were seen as prized possessions by the wrens in the various nests and seemed to give a nest with a baby in it a sense of higher status. If a child became sick it was taken to the workhouse as the doctor would not go to the bush. And the women that lived in the bush hated the thought of the workhouse as the conditions there were worse than the furze bushes of the Curragh.

All the takings of a nest were pooled, and the diet of potatoes, bread and milk was purchased on the few days when the women were allowed to attend the market in the camp. Otherwise it was out-of-bounds, but an army water-wagon brought them in a regular supply. Water was considered a luxury and every pint had to be paid for. The alternative was to drink the foul water collected on the plain. A wren named Mary Burns died through exposure and drinking the fetid water. Other luxuries were tea, tobacco and sugar.

Booze was popular too, especially whiskey and at night many of the wrens became heavily intoxicated and wild. Greenwood, being a conservative Victorian gentleman, was very distressed by this and was even quite frightened.

Following his visit to Kildare, Greenwood published a disturbing description of the condition of the women and, in the following year, when the *Curragh of Kildare Act* was passed it enabled the authorities to take action to regulate the use of the plains.

The gentleman at the *Pall Mall Gazette* decided that, contrary to popular belief, the women did not live in the furze because they were low-life creatures who revelled in debauchery. They were there because it was well known that those who were forced to seek refuge in the workhouse at Naas lived in even worse conditions, with rats, rampant disease and dangerous conditions. The poor souls who ended up there were treated horrifically by the brutal establishment who ran that cursed hellhole.

Those poor souls had no mercy shown to them by the authorities and especially the clergy. In November 1864, an article sometime attributed to Charles Dickens called 'Stoning the Desolate' appeared in his famous literary magazine *All the Year Round* (issue no. 292, 26 November 1864). The article narrated this powerful and damning story about a wren who was beaten by a priest. The account was given by an anonymous army officer, who had spent time at the Curragh. Dickens felt compelled to tell his tale as follows:

There are, in certain parts of Ireland and especially upon the Curragh of Kildare, hundreds of women, many of them brought up respectably, a few perhaps luxuriously, now living day-after-day, week-after-week, and month-after-month, in a state of solid heavy wretchedness, that no mere act of imagination can conceive. Exposed to sun and frost, to rain and snow, to the tempestuous east winds, and the bitter blast of the north, whether it be June or January, they live in the open air, with no covering but the wide vault of heaven, with so little clothing that even the blanket sent down out of heaven in a heavy fall of snow is eagerly welcomed by these miserable outcasts.

The misery that abounds round our large camps in England is a load heavy enough for us to bear, but it is not at all to be compared to what can be seen daily in Ireland. If one of these poor wretches were to ask but for a drop of water to her parched lips, or a crust of bread to keep her from starving, Christians would refuse it; were she dying in a ditch, they would not go near to speak to her of human sympathy, and of Christian hope in her last moments.

Yet, their priests preach peace on earth, good will among men, while almost in the same breath they denounce from their altars intolerant persecution against those who have, in many cases, been more sinned against than sinning. This is not a thing of yesterday. It has been going on for years, probably fifty, perhaps a hundred.

… Twenty years ago, in eighteen forty-four, I remember the priests coming into the barracks at Newbridge, with a request that the commanding officer would grant him a fatigue party of soldiers to go outside and pull down a few booths which these poor creatures had raised against the barrack wall. The priest, I am sorry to say, had his request granted, and at the head of the soldiers, on a cold winter's day, he went out and burned down the shelter these unfortunates had built. At this time it was quite common for the priest, when he met one of them, to seize her and cut her hair off close. But this was not all. In the summer of forty-five, a priest, meeting one of the women in the main street of Newbridge, there threw her down, tearing from off her back the thin shawl and gown that covered it, and with his heavy riding-whip so flogged her over the bare shoulders that the blood actually spirited over his boots. She all the time never resisted, but was only crying piteously for mercy.

Of the crowd that formed round the scene, not a man or a woman interfered by word or action. When it was over, not one said of the miserable soul, 'God help her.' Five days afterwards I saw this girl, and her back then was still so raw that she could not bear to wear a frock over it. Yet when she told me how it was done, and who did it, she never uttered a hard word against the ruffian who had treated her so brutally.

The author stated that if any person attacked an animal as savagely back in England, as the priest had beaten that poor girl, the strong arm of the law would have been stretched out between him and his victim.

He was disgusted that in Newbridge there was no one, man enough to take the law in his own hands, by seizing the whip from the priest and giving him on his own skin a lesson of mercy.

He felt that in Ireland, inhumanity of this sort was indeed encouraged; where shopkeepers and food suppliers considered it a part of religion not to supply these outcasts with the common necessaries of life; where the man who would dare allow one of them to crawl into his barn or cowshed to lie down and die, would be denounced from the altar, and be ordered to do penance for his charity. These were the author's words on the matter: 'I need not say, what is the result of this refusal of all Christian help and pity to the fallen'.

It seems that the officer who had passed on this account was aware of the corruption and darkness that enshrouded the Church long before anyone had the courage to challenge it, and it is only in recent years now that it has indeed been exposed.

Nellie Clifden

One particular Curragh wren, called Nellie Clifden, brought the British aristocracy into great disrepute.

From the seventeenth century, the Curragh Camp was a centre point for large numbers of military forces, including those serving during the Napoleonic wars. The first permanent buildings were erected there in 1855 in preparation for the Crimean War. It is still used to this day as a training ground for the Irish Army. In the mid-nineteenth century there were many soldiers living there and the Curragh Camp had developed a great reputation by then as a fine place to straighten out a young man, especially if he were showing signs of a wayward nature. There was a strict regime of routine and discipline and status did not mean one would get off lightly.

In 1861 it seemed like the perfect place to send the roughish nineteen-year-old Prince Albert (or more commonly known as Bertie to his friends) with the hope of knocking him into shape and maybe making a decent king out of him some day. He was sent for training with the Second Battalion of the Grenadier Guards (the most elite infantry regiment in the British Army), and his training was to last for ten weeks in total. He began his duties in

July of that year and it was suggested that he would be promoted every two weeks so that when his mother, Queen Victoria, came to visit she could witness her son commanding a battalion. It was hoped that this would give her some comfort and confidence in her wayward boy. The *Illustrated London News* tirelessly reported on the Prince as he went through the motions and promotions in fine detail.

On 24 August 1861, Victoria and Albert made a day trip to the Curragh Camp to see how their son was getting on. It was a fine day and the proud parents saw their son command his troops and watched as they carried out various battle formations, both on foot and on horseback, and displayed the loud and indeed frightening artillery. Albert even wrote to King William I of Prussia stating that Bertie did his part at the Curragh very well.

Unfortunately, what they did not take into consideration was the well hidden and secret sorority of wrens based in the plains of the Curragh. These fallen women were a major part of army extracurricular life. The stories have it that Bertie was no stranger to the wrens and indeed one wren in particular: Nellie Clifden.

Some said Nellie had been an actress and was well connected but had got herself into some sort of trouble and had sadly found herself among the sorority of lost souls known as the Curragh Wrens. One story stated that she had become pregnant by a soldier and had followed him to the Curragh only to be told by him that he wanted nothing more to do with her. She had no choice but to become one of the wrens. Nellie was a good-humoured and good-natured girl and the officers considered her the best of the wrens.

In gentlemen's clubs and stately mansions across Ireland and Britain, Nellie Clifden was about to become an extremely well-known name. Indeed, Nellie was to be brought before what was to be her most esteemed client – none other that Prince Albert, the Prince of Wales.

Nellie clearly impressed Bertie greatly, who became totally infatuated with her. Three nights later, she was summoned back for a second visit. And the following night, the young prince excitedly wrote 'NC, third time' in his diary.

But it was not long before word of the affair was to get out and jokes were starting to be told around the gentlemen's clubs about Nellie Clifden, 'The Princess of Wales'. Prince Albert's father was devastated by this news. His greatest fear was that the Irish girl would become pregnant and file a paternity suit against the prince, thereby destroying his son's chances of securing a wealthy European princess bride.

When Albert broke the news to Victoria, he spared her the 'disgusting details'. The couple agreed that, first and foremost, an early marriage was now essential or the prince would be 'lost'. Within three weeks of 'NC third time', Bertie was plucked from the Curragh and shipped to Germany where he was introduced to Princess Alexandra of Denmark. Albert and Victoria had determined she should be his future wife. Bertie was then enrolled at Cambridge University and placed under constant surveillance.

The entire affair might have blown over, but for Albert's decision to visit his rakish son in Cambridge. '*Bin recht elend*' (I feel miserable)' Bertie complained to his diary the day before they met. It was an emotional rain-swept encounter in which Albert forgave his son but warned that 'forgiveness could not restore the state of innocence and purity which (you have) lost forever'.

Three weeks later, on 14 December, Albert died. His death was said to be caused by typhoid fever. Later it was believed to be stomach cancer. However, for the grief-stricken Queen Victoria, it was quite clear that her beloved husband had died because of his shock at the carnal night, or nights, their son had spent with an Irish harlot. 'I never can or shall look at him without a shudder,' she wrote of Bertie. For the next forty years, Victoria openly and repeatedly treated her son and heir with utter contempt and did all she could to frustrate his ambitions. It is also believed that as a result of all this, Bertie was sent on many foreign expeditions, which were to become the royal tours that we know of today.

As for Nellie, her fate still remains anonymous. It was not known if she was paid off by the royal family, or worse, carefully dispatched under their orders. She may have changed her name and gone on to do greater things in the field of theatre and the arts. Or did the poor girl simply return to the grim furze bushes of the Curragh and lived out what was left of her life at the mercy of the soldiers. Apart from a popular racing mare cheekily named 'Miss Clifden' by one of Bertie's friends, Nellie's name and life story vanished from the archives. But the impact of her meeting with Bertie over 150 years ago would send ripples through the royal family long after her death.

Whatever the fate of Nellie Clifen and her fellow wrens, their memory lives on, and on a cold windy day in the middle of the Curragh plains if you listen very carefully you can still hear the mournful, lamenting sighs of the spirits of the Curragh wrens.

Nellie Clifden, what ever happened to you?
Vanquished, vilified, vanished
For you knew too much of what was true
Did they make you disappear,
Another victim of the great Royal fear?
Does your ghost still wander the Curragh Plain
Trapped in an eternal realm of shame?

A starving child clings to your breast
As you shelter inside a wild wren's nest,
Hiding from the terrible gale,
The howling winds
And the eternal rain,
Your body spent, exhausted and frail
As the night closes in around you.

Nellie Clifden what ever happened to you?
You came into this life
Your heart was pure and true.
Wide-eyed little girl, innocent and beautiful
Now your innocence has been taken away
And you would sell yourself for a penny
So that you might make it through the day.

Nellie when the prince took you in his arms
Did you fall for all his whispered charms?
Did you think this might be your chance
To laugh again, to sing and dance?
Did he promise to take you
From this terrible place
That robbed the smile from your face?

But fairy-tales are only make-believe
Sooner than later, they must take leave.
With only memories left to grieve,
Did you return to a wild wren's nest
And take your child back to your breast
Comforting her with a solemn lullaby
Nellie, did anyone ever answer your cries?

Steve Lally, 2014

15

MOLL ANTHONY
OF THE RED HILLS

While researching the folklore of County Kildare a name that kept cropping up was 'Moll Anthony'. Some people said she was a wise woman, some stated she was a type of medicine woman and others claimed she was a witch. When I heard this I was intrigued; every collector of folk tales loves to be told a tale about some class of a witch. As there are many tales surrounding this enigmatic character, I have tried to put together what I heard and read about her in order to tell you her story as best I can.

Moll Anthony, whose real name was Mary Leeson (*c.* 1807-1878), was an Irish *bean fasa* (wise woman) who lived at Hill of the Grange, between Milltown and Rathangan, but was originally from the Red Hills of County Kildare. She was named after her father, Anthony Dunne and lies buried in Milltown, County Kildare, where she died in 1878. There are two headstones beside each other in the cemetery, one of which states: 'Erected by Catherine Leeson of Grange Hill in memory of her dearly beloved husband, James Leeson who departed this life 27 April 1894, aged 64 years'.

Moll's stone states: 'Erected by Mary Leeson of Punchesgrange in memory of her mother, Eliza Cronley, who departed this life 11 December, 1851, aged 20 years. Also the above named Mary Leeson who died 28 November, 1878, aged 71 years'.

As the author Padraic O'Farrell pointed out in his book *Irish Fairy Tales* (1997) it would be impossible for Mary Leeson or 'Moll Anthony' who was born in 1807 to have a mother die at the age of 20 in 1851. There is a lot of speculation about this and some people in the area are still reluctant to talk about the stone. Indeed, when I went there to find the stone myself I was told by many of the locals that they did not know of such a headstone. And I was starting to doubt its existence until I did find it, but only after attending a rosary at Allan graveyard and lighting a prayer candle. When I returned I was compelled to walk straight to her headstone and was shocked to realise I had walked passed it so many times previously. Whether this is the final resting place of Moll Anthony of the Red Hills I cannot prove, but it certainly is where all the stories and research over the years has lead to.

There is one belief that Moll was born out of wedlock and the dates were tampered with to confuse those wishing to pass judgement. Nevertheless it remains a mystery, just like the character Moll Anthony herself.

One of the many stories surrounding Moll Anthony was about a sort of reincarnation of a young dead girl or a changeling left by the fairies to replace the young girl's body in her coffin.

The archeologist Lord Walter Fitzgerald (1858-1923) wrote about Moll Anthony in the *Kildare Archaeology Society Journal*, describing the strange way she arrived in Mullaghmast in the County Kildare. It goes something like this.

It was a cold and windy day and the leaves were being spun through the air like butterflies. The two sons of the widow Anthony, who lived near Mullaghmast, met a funeral party on the road. As was the custom at the time, the two boys followed the cortege and even helped to carry the coffin. When the cortege arrived at the front of their house the pallbearers put down the coffin and walked off into the distance, disappearing into an ethereal mist. The boys, terrified, ran into the house and told their mother. She came out and opened the coffin, to discover a young girl there, warm and breathing gently as if sleeping. The girl recovered and she grew up with the family for the next nine years. According to Fitzgerald, the widow decided to call her Mary, a straightforward name but one with tenacity. From that day for each of the nine years, Mary was a great help to the widow Anthony. She happily did the house-work and menial chores around the place. Good luck and prosperity seemed to have entered the house with her, and the farm thrived as it had never done before.

One day at the end of the nine years, the widow Anthony said to her elder son, 'Jim, it would be no harm in life if ye had the dacency to ask that gerrel if she wanted to be buried with our people and you make a dacent woman of her'.

'Oh! Be-God and be the Tear O' War,' replied Jim. 'Do ya know I was tinkin' o' dat meself, shur good-luck is better nor any fortune at all, so it is.' In the end the two were married and by the time the three children were crawling about the house, Jim said he would have to go to Castledermot to buy a filly. 'I have never asked the like afor Jim,' said Mary, 'but I'm wishful to go wid ye.'

'Shur you are more than welcome, sweet Mary,' said Jim. 'Shure me mother will mind the childher.'

So off they went in the ass-cart, and arrived at the fair. Seeing a suitable filly in the charge of a young lad, Jim bid to within

£5 of the price asked for it, and was referred to the owner, who was in the town with his wife. When they met, Jim and his wife Mary invited the couple to a public house to settle the deal. Noticing that the old man was staring hard at Mary after the bargain was clinched, Jim asked, 'What in the blazes are ye lookin' in that unmannerly way at me woman for?'

'Well now,' said the old man, 'if it wasn't as certain as I have the price of the filly in me breeches pocket, I'd take me oath that that was me own daughter – the Lord have mercy on her! I buried her some years ago.'

'Can ye give me the day and date?' says Jim.

'If I can't, herself can,' says he, looking over at his wife, whom he called over to his aid. She was so wrapped up in the gossip and craic going on in the establishment that she had not paid much attention to Mary in the way her husband had and answered the question without hesitation.

'It was 3 May, thirteen year ago,' says she.

'Oh! Be the Tear O' War, that's fierce queer indeed,' says Jim. 'Shure that's the very day I first laid me eye on me woman.'

Looking at Mary, the old woman said to her, 'Come to the parlour wid me, alanna and I'll soon know if himself there is right'.

'Arrah, mother,' said Mary, 'don't trouble to see me stripped, shure I'll not deny that the raspberry mark is on me shoulder.'

'Glory be to god, it's true,' said the old woman. And that was how Mullaghmast became ingratiated with the presence of Moll Anthony.

Some things are most peculiar and this was one of them indeed. And it may be explained by the belief in the power of the fairies to carry off a person and leave a behind a substitute, resembling them in every way, manner and form, but concealing hidden powers. These were known as changelings and it was widely considered that Moll Anthony was such a creature. This too would give good weight to the belief that she had dealings with 'the good people', 'the children of Danu' or 'the fairies'.

It was well known that Moll Anthony of the Red Hills had a supernatural power for curing paralysis, fits, strokes and other sicknesses in both humans and animals. It was said that she got the gift from the good people or the fairies. Sometimes, however, she would refuse to help a person or animal, if she thought it best for the person or beast to die, or if it was their second time of seeking her help. It was also stated that before stricken people had a chance to introduce themselves and describe their symptoms, she would welcome the complete strangers by addressing them by their name and telling them their sickness.

Moll cured both people and animals with potions she created from particular herbs. Each potion was given in three separate porter bottles, two of which she gave on her first visit, the third bottle being given on the second visit. The charge was half a crown per bottle.

There were very strict rules applied to the administration, consumption and transportation of these powerful potions, and if any of the rules weren't adhered to, the cure failed. A cure was never allowed to be used twice. So magical and powerful was the cure, that on bringing it home, the bearer was often stalled by some evil spirit, who would try and stop them from reaching their destination. This in itself was a great deterrent for people who wished to avail of Moll's expertise, and proved that there was a lot more to her skills than mere knowledge of herbs and medicine. It was definitely a hazardous affair when you decided to take help from Moll Anthony. However, if the doses were correctly administered, a cure was always successful. So, depending on the seriousness of the ailment and how precious that person or beast was considered, it was sometimes worth the high risks involved.

Fitzgerald recorded a story about one such treacherous journey, involving two men, William Whelan of Ballyvass, who died age seventy-two in 1901, and Simon Gleeson of Castleroe, who died aged eighty-five in 1909. These two individuals were given strict orders by Moll Anthony not to delay in any shape or form on their road home. She also made it very clear that they were to travel on foot, no matter what the distance was they had to travel. The bottles were to be kept on their person at all times and if they rested or fell asleep along the way the bottles were sure to be removed from them by some malevolent spirit or entity. Moll warned the men that at a certain place about three quarters of a mile from her home along the road a terrible fatigue would test their will-power to carry on and stay awake. If they dozed off or stopped to speak with anyone they met, the bottles would be lost forever.

And when the men reached this place that Moll had spoken of a great sense of exhaustion and weariness overcame the men. They experienced a terrible pain in their feet and a great desire to sleep. They wanted to take off their boots and relieve their aching feet, but to do this would only slow them down and cause more discomfort on the hard, cold, stony road. As bad as this first journey was, the return journey was according to the men, twice as bad. They experienced wild voices and laughter. They felt a terrible presence about them and an awful sense of foreboding. They found themselves crawling on their hands and knees, trying to get past that cursed area about which Moll had warned them.

When they were lucky enough to get back in one piece that was not the end of it. They still had to administer the cure. The dose for a human (a young girl of ten in this case) patient was always three teaspoonfuls out of the first bottle and after a twenty-four-hour period three more tea-spoon-fuls from the second bottle. A part of the liquid, too, had to be rubbed on the palms of the hands and the soles of the feet of the poor patient. This all went very smoothly and without any drama or distraction. On the arrival of the third bottle (for which the second visit was necessary) a similar dose was prescribed after another twenty-four hours. In the meantime it was imperative that this third bottle was kept well guarded, preferably locked away somewhere safe until it was time for the final dose to come. This had to be done as the patient would become possessed by some terrible spirit or demon and try to smash the bottle and destroy its contents. When the time came to administer the potion, the poor child resisted violently while the teaspoonfuls were being given to her. She twisted and turned and yelled all sorts of terrible obscenities. Having been advised to have a priest present, the girl was also dosed in holy water.

What added to the difficulty and drama of this situation was the fact that none of the liquid was to be spilt if the cure was to be in any way effective. Luckily this was done but not without great struggle and complexity. What was then left of the mixture after the third and final dose was to be taken out of the house and thrown against the wind, and so scattered in such a way that it could not be trodden upon or walked over.

Any accidents or carelessness involving spilling the liquid would render the cure ineffective and it was a waste of time to journey back to Moll Anthony as she would never pre-scribe a second time for the same case.

The three doses were absolutely necessary for the cure to work and there were occasions where after the first two the patient seemed totally recovered and the second journey to see Moll was not made, much to the relief of those given the task to do so. The result for this complacency was that the patient became very ill again or they became what was then described as 'An Innocent' or 'Harmless Simpleton'. Thankfully according to the two men the cure worked and the girl was as good as new.

Not all these excursions were as successful. There was a young woman who travelled from a neighbouring county to see Moll in the Red Hills of Kildare. A relative of hers was very ill. Moll gave her the strange potion to bring back and told her to keep her eyes open on the way home. After the girl had walked a fair distance and covered most of the journey she became very tired. It was as if her feet had turned to lead and she wanted so desperately to sit and rest, but she had been warned by Moll not to stop under any circumstances at all. She could take it no longer and sat down by the side of a ditch to rest her weary bones. All of a sudden a horrible, wrinkled old hag with no teeth, a nose like a beak and a ferocious contorted face came towards her at great speed. She seemed to fly through the air. She had a pair of very long outstretched skinny arms like great spiders' legs swiping around, trying to grab the poor girl. The hag was howling like a Banshee and the girl got such a fright that she jumped to her feet and as she did so, the precious bottle fell to the ground and smashed into pieces. When the girl did eventually get home, she found her sick relative cold and lifeless on their bed.

Not all of Moll Anthony's work was considered for the greater good. According to Kathleen Coffey, who wrote about the wise woman, it was believed that Moll was in cahoots with 'Auld Nick' or the Devil. This was recorded in the National Folklore Collection held at University College Dublin.

It was said that Moll often cast charms and spells over those who she saw as her enemies, or over those who injured her

in any way, either by word or deed. As a result of this Moll Anthony was seen as a witch or fairy doctor, and struck a combination of awe, respect and terror in those who knew her. In her book, *Wise Woman of Kildare*, Erin Kraus states that Moll Anthony was largely left alone, unless her help was needed.

As well as her cures, Moll also made money from hexes, offering her services to those who wished to seek revenge or settle a score. She was Ireland's very own Marie Laveau, the infamous Voodoo Queen of New Orleans. Not only was Moll considered a witch doctor or fairy doctor but she was also considered as '*bean feasa*' or wise woman. Now this was indeed a highly recognised and revered status. For a wise woman was believed to have powers far beyond what ordinary folk have and can even see into the future, like the oracles of Greek mythology. She was on communication terms with the fairies and their ancient wisdom and their power worked through her. She was a force to be reckoned with, and no one would dare cross her if they knew of her status and abilities.

The most common help sought from Moll Anthony was in regard to the theft of goods and loss of profit. An eighty-four-year-old man called William Byrne from Kilranlagh, Killegan, County Wicklow, talked a lot about the stories that he heard as a child about Moll Anthony. He describes in the National Folklore Collection how people used to go to her to get their sick animals cured and their profits back. He talked about a boy who was unable to make butter after a strange old woman came begging on a May morning and must have put some hex upon the buttermilk. Another story describes how a farmer with six or eight cows could not produce butter, while a neighbour with only one cow had an abundant supply of the stuff and finally another farmer suspected that his butter was being stolen. All three went to

Moll Anthony to put an end to their troubles. The advice she gave to the three men was identical. She said to them: 'Next time you are churning, put the chains of the plough around the churn; put the coulter of the plough in the fire, make it red hot and then plunge it into the churn, when the butter should be forming. In all three cases, once the coulter was plunged into the churn, the profit thief came running to the window or door, screaming in agony, and butter was plentiful in their households from that moment onwards.

Many stories and recollections suggest that Moll Anthony passed on her 'cures' to members of her family. Through research and piecing together stories about her, it was possible to trace the existence of healers from Moll's family right up to the 1930s. Fitzgerald mentions in a 1915 article that 'the cure' was still in possession of Moll Anthony's grandson's (James Leeson) widow, who still resided at the time in a comfortable slated house on the Hill of Grange. There were records in the National Folklore Collection of 1937-8 stating that a Mrs Leeson of the Red Hills, Rathangan 'has a cure for everything'. Another reference describes a Mrs Leeson who lived on the Hill of Grange and inherited the cure from an ancestor. Another woman around that same time known for her cures was called Mrs Gleeson but known to the locals as 'Moll Anthony'. As these references were made by children, spelling was not a top priority and similarities in name are not mere coincidence.

There is wonderful little story recorded by Patrick Kennedy in his book *Fictions of the Irish Celts* (Macmillan & Co., 1866).

> The neighbourhood of Borraheen, Baltracy and Rathcoffey was blessed,
> or the contrary, in times past, by a fortuneteller and charm-concocter,

Moll Anthony by name. So unedifying was her life and conversation, that the priest refused to have any religious services performed for her after her death. She left a son, who had acquired some skill in curing cattle by herbs, and did not pretend to any Supernatural gifts.

A farmer, Pat Behan, at whose house he had remained about a fortnight, and who was well pleased with his performances, was passing near the green hills in his jaunting car, accompanied by Jack Anthony, the doctor, when, on the sudden, an old woman in a red cloak appeared to them between the bushes and the road-fence, and cried 'Jack, it's time for you to come!'.

'Sir', said Jack to his patron, 'Will you excuse me for a minute, while I go to say a word to this neighbour of mine.'

'Oh! To be sure Jack,' replied the farmer. Jack got on the fence and passed through the bushes, but the farmer was surprised at not subsequently hearing the sound of his or her voice. He waited for about the space of a minute, and then bade his servant to climb the fence, and see if Jack was about to return. The servant did as he was told, and the master observed him look along the inner side of the ditch, now to the left, and then to the right, and then straight before him, with a perplexed expression on his face. The master sprung down, joined his servant, and found he had a long range of vision right and left, and up to the sloping side of the Green Hill, and no bushes or rocks to afford concealment. Neither Jack nor the red-cloaked woman, were in view. It was months before the doctor presented himself before his patron, and even then his account of his disappearance was not consistent in all its parts.

I suppose we will never know what happened to Jack when he disappeared with the strange woman and one can only assume that she was his own dear mother, Moll Anthony.

After that there is not much known about the legacy of the illustrious Moll Anthony. However, I myself remember that some twenty years ago, when my father was terminally ill with cancer and all the medical wonders of modern science were rendered useless against his condition, it was suggested that my father go and see a wise woman somewhere in a remote part of Kildare where he was given a strange concoction that was kept in an old milk bottle in the fridge. I remember it stank like hell and I am sure it tasted worse. It seemed to ease my father's pain, but unfortunately could not save him. Still I wonder who this person was who administered the strange concoction and whether they are still alive and maybe even descended from Moll Anthony? Well, that will be another story to tell.

16

POLL THE PISHOGUE

After writing about Moll Anthony of the Red Hills I was introduced to another enigmatic Kildare character who went under the name of Poll the Pishogue.

A pishogue is an old Irish word for a spell or witchcraft. It was very much associated with the concept of creating a spell to cure or even cause illness to both beasts and humans. Now the name Poll could be derived from the Irish for hole. In old Ireland it was greatly believed that 'the good people' or 'the fairies' lived below the earth in holes. In fact, there is a place in County Wicklow called Pollaphouca, and translated means 'hole of the pooka'.

The pooka was a solitary and sinister fairy who has most likely never appeared in human form. His shape is usually that of a horse, bull, goat, eagle or donkey. But most commonly he takes the form of a horse and he enjoys throwing unwary riders onto their backs on the ground, as well as taking them over ditches, rivers and mountains, and shakes them off in the early grey-light of the morning.

So one might say that Poll the Pishogue was, at the very least, an unusual character. I found this story from Con Costello's book Kildare: Saints, Soldiers and Horses, published by the Leinster Leader in 1919. This is her story.

In 1840 Mr and Mrs C.S. Hall, in their *Ireland – Its Scenery & Character*, magazine gave a detailed description of their visit to Poll the Pishogue, who lived in a hut made of turf in the Bog of Allen: 'Nothing could exceed in misery the appearance of her hovel raised something in the form of a cone'.

Her goat grazed on the grass that sprang from the roof as on the herbage by which it was surrounded. A deep trench encircled this turf edifice on all sides and a narrow log of bog oak was laid across it, opposite the door, which enabled Poll's visitors to 'Pass and repass with all the comfort and ease of life' as she would say. The inside of this strange, almost otherworldly abode consisted of one room and when the interior was not so full of smoke, and a stranger could both see and breathe, it was not so bad and it was warm and dry, for while the rain could enter in one or two places, it could run out as quickly as it came in. Poll had a bed and plenty of wooden stools and bosses (small straw stools). But what was quite impressive was the fact that she had managed to install a glass window and a cupboard containing crockery and two strange-looking green bottles. In these Poll had what she referred to as, 'Only a sup of eye-water, a wash for the hives and a cure (god bless it) for the chincough.'

The bottles' contents smelt of whiskey and when asked about the contents Poll replied, 'Hard for them to help it, when the spirits is the foundation of every cure. Herbs dear! Sent by the grace of God, which I gather fasting under bames [beams] of the full moon and steeps [soaked or marinated] – oh, nothing else, only according to knowledge'.

As Poll's hut was near the canal it was common for people to come by boat or barge to visit her in order to get some relief from whatever was ailing them. People who did not have this means of transport would walk or travel by horse and cart for miles to get to see Poll the Pishogue. She was indeed a well-renowned wise woman and both revered and feared by those who knew her.

There are many tales about Poll and what she did but one that stands out is about a young woman and a baby who was terribly sick. In fact, there was a good chance that the poor little child was going to die. So the young mother brought the child to see Poll in her hut out in the middle of the Bog of Allen.

Poll told her to sit down on one of the wee stools in her hovel. The young woman told Poll that she nailed a horse-shoe to her door and put plenty of salt about the place to keep it safe from evil spirits and unwanted visits from the fairy folk, but her child was still wasting away and the skin was hanging from its bones. She was sure that the child was a changeling left behind by the fairies, and it was not her own babe at all. Poll comforted the woman by telling her that the child was not a changeling and the woman gave Poll a few half-pence for her help. Poll then asked if her baby had been kept away from the 'shop-doctors' (meaning the dispensary or local general practice doctor). The woman assured Poll that she had every faith in her cure and would not be going to any quacks. She had a charm around the baby's neck and said that all was well other than her husband had no regular work for the past two months and they had to halve their rations of food, but their neighbours were no better off than them. But she also told Poll that the poor cat had died from starvation as there was no milk. It was quite obvious for anyone looking in at that bizarre encounter that the poor little infant too was dying from starvation. The woman, however, seemed pretty satisfied that whatever was wrong with the baby, Poll's cure would surely rectify it.

Now Poll was a bit annoyed with the woman because she had not brought a bottle with her to carry home the potion. Poll, reluctantly, gave her a small jar containing the cure and told the mother to cross the baby's breast with the liquid every evening while the sun was getting ready to set. What happened to the family is not known, but one would like to think that the woman's husband did some work, and that there was food coming into the house and one would like to believe that the faith the woman had brought fortune. One might argue why did the woman not use the money she spent on the cure for food for her child, but we have to remember that many rural people were of a very primitive nature in old Ireland and superstition and belief in otherworldly powers carried more weight than what was happening in the world around them.

Poll had a fear of priests who did not approve of her cures and methods. But she claimed that she never dealt in the black arts, beyond the sowing of hemp-seed or placing a shirt to air at the fire, in the devil's name. She possessed a powerful murrain stone, far superior to the one owned by the 'markiss' as she liked to call him. This 'markiss' or marquis was Lord Waterford, and this magical stone was believed to have been brought back to Ireland in ancient times from the Levant, a term used to describe the eastern Mediterranean, including such places as Greece, Turkey parts of the Holy Lands and Lebanon. Poll was a great teller of the meanings behind birthmarks and moles. She did not believe in the use of 'the dead man's hand' for that was very much part of the practice of black magic. Poll was noted for her powers of prediction, her love-potions, matchmaking and her many pishogues.

She had a keen eye, and was hard featured, resembling a witch in all the classical descriptions of one. She had a black cat with wild green eyes. She was held in awe by the peasantry of the time. Nobody would dare cross her, for they were terrified of a terrible curse being put upon them. Whether she

was a real witch or not is not known but she certainly had all the hallmarks of one and if one was to come across her little conical hut made of turf sod and the smoke billowing out of it in the heart of the Bog of Allen they would not be overly surprised to see Poll arriving at the door on a broomstick.

17

THE TRINITY
WELL

*A holy well is a spring or other water source that for one reason or
another is considered to be holy or sacred. Many of these wells were
used in pre-Christian rituals and are often called Saint Brigid's
wells. What is interesting about them is that fairy trees often
grow very close to them and they seem to share a common ground
together. These wells are still believed to have healing powers and
are frequented by many people today. One in particular is still
frequented by pilgrims every Sunday in Kildare. This well is
known as 'The Trinity Well'. I found this story in a great little
book entitled* The Holy Wells of Ireland, *by Patrick Logan,
published by Colin Smythe Ltd, 1980.*

The River Boyne rises in a pool, now known as Trinity
Well, near Carbury, County Kildare; a popular pilgrimage
is made to this well on Trinity Sunday. The story goes that a
king called Nechtan lived at Carbury Hill (Sidh Nechtain),
and had in his garden a very special well, which no woman
might approach or take water from. Despite this, Boan,
the wife of Nechtan, not only approached the well, but
insulted it gravely by walking three times round it in an
anti-clockwise direction. This was considered blasphemous

to the gods. At the insult the well rose up and like a tidal wave came after her. As she fled hysterically, the water formed a river as she ran and it was named after Queen Boan – the River Boyne. Eventually the water caught up with her and swept her out to sea, and she was drowned.

The pre-Christian Irish worshipped the River Boyne as a goddess and clearly this story is derived from their religious beliefs. In 1849, William Wilde, father of the poet and writer Oscar Wilde, wrote *The Beauties of the Boyne and its Tributary the Blackwater*. In it he writes about a number of other holy wells that are found close to the young river and add their waters to it. These are now as completely Christianised as Trinity Well. The first is Tobercro (Tobar Croiche Naoimh – The Well of the Holy Cross). Wilde then mentioned the Beautiful Well and next to it Lady Well, where he said that a pattern was held early in the nineteenth century. Wilde also mentioned two others, Carbury Well and Tobar na Cille – 'six in all, baptising the infant Boyne'. Of course the Boyne is heavily associated with the Battle of the Boyne of 1690 and is celebrated every year by the Orange Order on 12 July. So it seems that this river transcended many changes in religious beliefs over the centuries.

18

QUEEN
BUAN

This is a story that is very close to my heart as I heard it when I was a small boy. Little did I know it would have a direct relation to my own father who sadly passed away and rests at Mainham graveyard in Clane, County Kildare. Overlooking the ancient graveyard of Mainham stands the burial mound of 'Queen Buan' the Queen of Leinster and pride of the Celtic people. This is her story.

On the outskirts of the village of Clane, County Kildare, lies a townland called Mainham, beside Clongowes Wood College, the former residence of a family named Browne. Here there is a cemetery known to all the locals as 'Mainham graveyard'. This graveyard holds many of the secrets and stories of Ireland. It houses the remains of an early-Christian monastery, a Norman church, graves from the great plantation period and a lonely mausoleum which stands just outside the churchyard wall, which contains a vault in which members of the Browne family who died during the seventeenth and eighteenth centuries have been buried. Inside is an effigy of a shrouded figure with two death heads looming over it. A limestone altar stands at the rear wall with kneeling

figures carved into it. There are the scattered graves of many
people who gave their lives in the struggle for freedom in
Ireland. But the most ancient and breath-taking of all these
markers of history is a great Celtic burial mound that looms
over the graveyard in an adjoining field. It is overgrown with
grass and trees and is home to all sorts of wildlife. This magnificent mound is known locally as the burial mound of
Queen Buan. Queen Buan was the wife of Mesgegra, King
of Leinster who lived at Naas (Nas na Rí). She was buried
separately from her husband the king, whose remains lie in
another mound at Clane, also in Kildare. Both their stories
hold all the hallmarks of a great Celtic tragedy. This is how
it began.

In ancient Ireland there dwelt a cruel, merciless man
called Atherne the Urgent of Ulster. He was a persistent and
unrelenting poet-druid. He was the sort of man that asked
a one-eyed man for his single eye and would not thank him
for it.

He was called upon by King Cochobar (Conor) Mac
Nessa, the King of Ulster's counsel, to go on a (bardic)
circuit of Ireland. He went west around Ireland till he made
the round of Connaught. He then went to the king of
the middle of Ireland, between the two Fords of Hurdles,
to Eochaid son of Luchta, king of the south of Connaught.
Eochaid then took the poet Atherne to the King of Munster
over the Shannon, in a southward direction.

Atherne, being a poet of great power, demanded great
respect amongst the royalty of Ireland and he abused this
power. He ordered that he should take the King of Munster's
queen for himself for one night or else he would create a
damning poem about the king and the men of Munster.
By doing this he would take away their honour and respect
from the other kingdoms. The poor queen offered herself to

cruel Atherne, for the sake of her husband's honour, and the honour of her people.

Atherne then went to Leinster, and stopped in Ard Brestine in the south of Moyfea. He was offered jewels and treasures not to come into the country, so that he might not leave behind damning poems about them. He was not impressed at all with the gifts that were brought to him by the local king's representatives – in fact he laughed in their faces. The people threatened to slay him for his insults and he laughed at them again, stating that if they did kill him, Ulster would be forever avenging him on Leinster. He stated that he would leave an *ail bréthre* (verbal insult) on them for ever, so that they should not hold up their faces before the Gael, unless they gave him the jewel that was best on the Hill of Allen; and he said that no one knew what this jewel was or what place it was in upon the hill.

This was an outrage and a great disgrace to the hosts of Leinster. And they all called upon the Lord of the Elements to give them help to avenge this outrage that was inflicted upon them.

So the people took Atherne to the Hill of Allen where they watched a horseman training his horse on the hill. As he was galloping fiercely across the hill, the horse flung a great sod from his two hooves. No one in the meeting noticed it till it fell into lap of the king, Fergus Fairge. Sticking out from the sod, he saw a brooch made of solid red gold and encrusted with the finest jewels and with the finest craftsmanship worked into the precious metal. 'What is this that has fallen into my lap, Atherne?' said the king.

'That is the jewel that I spoke of,' said Atherne. 'My father's brother ripped it from a slayed warrior, and buried it in the ground during a bloody battle against the Ulstermen.'

So then the brooch was given to him and the people were relieved to see him go. He then went to see Mesgegra, the king of Leinster. Mesgegra made great welcome to Atherne, and did his best to make him feel at ease, but the cruel and malevolent bard was not interested because he had already decided what he wanted. He demanded that he take all the women of the king's court with him, including Mesgegra's beautiful wife, Queen Buan.

King Mesgegra refused and Queen Buan and all her ladies-in-waiting were taken to the Bog of Allen for safety. The Leinsterman and their king then chased Atherne from Kildare. But the Ulstermen came to protect Atherne and a brutal battle was fought.

The Ulstermen were sent into retreat, and they fled by the sea eastward until they were trapped in Howth. Nine days and nights they were in Howth without drink, or food, unless they drank the brine of the sea, or they devoured the clay.

The Leinstermen waited patiently and then attacked. It was a vicious and ruthless slaughter. The women were returned home safely, but that was not to be the end of it.

A great and fierce Ulster warrior called Conall Cernach lost two of his brothers in the fighting and to avenge them he pursued the King of Leinster, whom he confronted in Clane. He found King Mesgegra with one of his servants. The king had just lost his hand as the result of a quarrel. Conall therefore fought Mesgegra with one hand tucked in his belt to make it a fair fight. He defeated Mesgegra and cut off his head, which he then placed on a sacred Bullaun stone at the edge of the ford in Clane County Kildare. (In another version of the story he placed the head on another stone and the blood was so powerful it ate away through the stone like acid and went through it. Some of the blood hit Conall in the eye and made him go cross-eyed). The Bullaun stone was believed to have been used for human sacrifice, and it is still there today.

It can be found opposite the Franciscan Friary in Clane, beside the Butterstream.

Conall then took the head and placed it on his own and covered himself up with a great cloak and mounted his chariot taking the servant with him and made his way to see Queen Buan, whom he wished to take for himself under the pretence that he was indeed her husband Mesgegra. As he rode towards Mainham, Mesgegra's wife, Buan (which means 'eternal'), was waiting anxiously for her husband's arrival, and Conall called out to her under the pretext that the words came from Mesgegra's mouth. She was so happy and relieved to see her husband returning that she ran to him. But then Conall revealed his true self by removing Mesgegra's head from his own. When Queen Buan witnessed this horrific sight she screamed so loud that her heart burst and she fell dead to the ground.

Unmoved by this, Conall then tried to take hold of the head again, but it was impossible to lift. Then he said to his servant, 'Take out the brains with your sword, take them away and mix them with earth to make a ball for a sling.' This was known as a brain-ball or *Tathlum*, meaning a concrete ball, and was made by mixing human brains with lime and allowing it to harden. These were ritualistic weapons used to kill powerful foes. Balor of the Baleful Eye was said to have been killed with a *Tathlum*. The ancient Celts being headhunters believed that the heads of their enemies contained great powers and strength so to make a missile using the brain was a formidable weapon.

This ball was then exhibited in the hall of the Bloody Branch or Red Branch. One day, when the Ulstermen were drunk and King Conchobar (King Conor Mac Nessa could not restore peace among them) ordered that the 'brains of Mesgegra' be brought to him. This inspired such

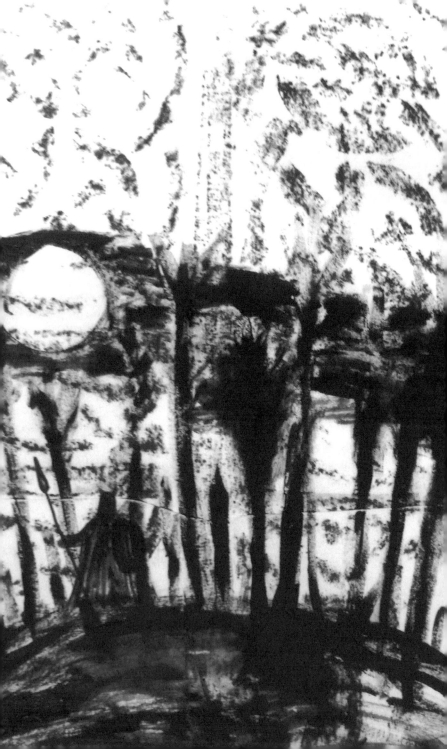

terror that when he challenged the other warriors to single combat with stone and sling no one would oppose him, and the 'brains' were put away again, with harmony and brotherhood restored.

But Cet, son of Maga, a great warrior from Leinster, who was always in search of an evil deed (an Ulsterman's head to cut off), knowing that Mesgegra had predicted that his death would be avenged by his own head, seized the 'brains' and managed to throw them at King Conchobar's head with great force. It embedded itself in Conchobar skull. His doctor refused to remove the ball and would only tie it to him with a golden thread. King Conchobar was greatly disabled by this and could only remain seated in his throne and watch the others. After seven years he lost his temper, the 'Brain of Mesgegra' burst from his head, and he died.

He was later avenged by Conall Cernach, who killed Cet, Son of Maga, and cut off his head. And Conall Cernach himself met his own death many years later at the hands of the men of Connaught.

The remains of King Mesgegra were buried in a mound in Clane where he had met his death.

Queen Buan was buried at the mound in Mainham on the outskirts of Clane. Like her name, her memory is eternal and she still keeps watch over the souls of Mainham graveyard, a silent sentry who died of a broken heart.

19

LANIGAN'S BALL

No collection of folk tales about Kildare would be complete without including the great Kildare folk song, Lanigan's Ball. This chapter is dedicated to Ray Dunne from Athy, County Kildare, and my co-founder of The Quiet Men, a new venture celebrating the ancient art of the Bard and the Storyteller.

It is still one of my all-time favourites and warms my heart every time I hear it and sure, what man or woman alive would not feel compelled to dance to 'Lanigan's Ball'?

'Lanigan's Ball' (sometimes 'Lannigan's Ball') is a popular traditional or folk Irish song that has been played throughout the world since at least the 1860s and possibly much longer. Typically performed in a minor key, it is generally played in an upbeat style reminiscent of the party atmosphere of the story unfolding through the lyrics.

The lyrics are about a party thrown by a hardworking young man, Jeremy Lanigan, who has inherited a 'farm and ten acres of ground' on the death of his father. The events occur in Athy, County Kildare. Jeremy decides to have the party for friends and relations who supported and helped

him out when he didn't have any resources; 'friends and relations who didn't forget him when come to the wall'.

The lyrics of the song describe the people who attended
the party and the food and drink that was available. In the
chorus of the song, the narrator describes his time spent at
'Brooks Academy' in Dublin learning to dance in preparation
for the ball:

> In the town of Athy one Jeremy Lanigan
> Battered away till he hadn't a pound
> And his father he died and made him a man again,
> Left him a farm and ten acres of ground.
> He gave a grand party to friends and relations
> Who did not forget him when come to the wall.
> If you'd only listen, I'll make your eyes glisten
> At the rows and ructions of Lanigan's Ball.

> Six long months I spent in Dublin,
> Six long months doing nothing at all.
> Six long months I spent in Dublin,
> Learning to dance for Lanigan's ball.

> Myself to be sure got free invitations
> For all the nice girls and boys I might ask.
> In less than a minute both friends and relations
> We're dancing as merry as bees round a cask.
> Lashings of punch and wine for the ladies,
> Potatoes, cakes, there was bacon and tea.
> There were the Nolans, Dolans, O'Gradys,
> Courting the girls and dancing away.

> Six long months I spent in Dublin,
> Six long months doing nothing at all.

Six long months I spent in Dublin,
Learning to dance for Lanigan's ball.

They were doing all kinds of nonsensical polkas
Round the room in a whirly gig
But Julia and I soon banished their nonsense
And tipped them a twist of a real Irish jig.
Oh how the girl she really got mad and we
Danced that you'd think that the ceiling would fall,
For I spent three weeks at Brooks Academy
Learning to dance for Lanigan's ball.

Six long months I spent in Dublin,
Six long months doing nothing at all.
Six long months I spent in Dublin,
Learning to dance for Lanigan's ball.

And I stepped out – and I stepped in again
Learning to dance for Lanigan's ball
The boys were as merry, the girls all hearty,
Dancing around in couples and groups.
Till an accident happened, young Terence McCarthy
He put his right leg through Miss Finerty's hoops.
The creature she fainted and cried 'Meelia Murther'
And called for her brothers and gathered them all.
Carmody swore that he'd go no further,
Till he had satisfaction at Lanigan's ball.

Six long months I spent in Dublin,
Six long months doing nothing at all.
Six long months I spent in Dublin,
Learning to dance for Lanigan's ball.

Boys, oh boys, tis there was ructions
Myself got a kick from big Phelim McHugh
And I soon replied to his kind introduction
And kicked him a terrible hullabaloo.
Casey the piper was nearly being strangled,
They squeezed up his pipes, bellows, chanters and all
And the girls in their ribbons they all got entangled
And that put an end to Lanigan's ball.

Six long months I spent in Dublin,
Six long months doing nothing at all.
Six long months I spent in Dublin,
Learning to dance for Lanigan's ball.
And I stepped out – and I stepped in again
Learning to dance for Lanigan's ball.

20

THE DEATH COACH

This is a great story that I found in the 1902 edition of the Kildare Archaeological Society Journal. *The story was told by a man called Tom Daly from Millbrook in Rathangan, County Kildare and was collected by Miss Greene. I have other accounts that claim the same Death Coach was seen in and around Mullaghmast, near Athy in Kildare. I have put together all the information that I found to present you with this spine-chilling tale.*

Tom Daly was going home one night from wherever it was he had been. He was a private sort a man and minded his own business. He never had any issue with walking the quiet, lonely roads at night by himself as he had no belief in the strange stories that people would tell around the fire at night. That was all about to change.

Tom reckoned that it was around midnight, when he was just at the top of 'Sal's Hill', that he heard a loud buzzing noise coming towards him. Then he saw something approaching him at a ferocious speed. According to Tom, it was speeding up 'The Long Acre', or 'The Ditch' as it is more commonly known. His heart was in his mouth with the fear. At first he thought it was one of

those newfangled motorcars that were causing so many disturbances around the countryside. But what on earth was is doing in The Ditch? Also, no vehicle then would have been able to travel at such a great speed.

It was buzzing like a thresher and creating an awful noise. He said that there were no lights and he couldn't see the shape of it behind the hedge. Tom stepped out into the middle of the road to try and get a better look at what this strange contraption was and he realised it was a type of coach. He stood and looked at it as it went down to the quarry lane, but then poor Tom got the fright of his life when he saw that the men driving the coach had no heads and the horses pulling it were headless also. The coach then disappeared into the night.

Tom claimed he never saw it again but he did hear the whirring, buzzing sound of 'The Death Coach' a few times more in and around the area.

There is speculation that this phantom carriage was associated with a terrible massacre that took place in Mullamast in 1577, when the chiefs of Uí Failghe and Laoighis were lured into a trap and massacred by the O'Dempseys and their English allies. There is a deep hollow in the ground where the slaughter was supposed to have taken place and it is known as 'The Bloody Hole'.

Lord Walter Fitzgerald, in his article in *The Kildare Archaeological Society Journal* from 1895 entitled 'Mullaghmast, its Histories and Traditions', reproduces a memorial drawn up by Captain Thomas Lee in 1594. It written was for presentation to Queen Elizabeth I, and argued that the country was being misgoverned and the native Irish were being treated. In it he says:

> They have drawn unto them, by protection, three or four hundred of those country people, under Colour to do your Majesty service,

and brought them to a place of meeting, where your garrison soldiers were appointed to be, who have there most dishonourably put them all to the sword; and this hath been by the consent and practice of the Lord Deputy for the time being. If this be a good course to draw these savage people to the state to do your Majesty service, and not rather to enforce them to stand upon their guard, I humbly leave to your Majesty.

21

Kildare
Fairy Tales

These stories are included in the National Folklore Collection held at the Newman Building at University College Dublin. The collection consists of folklore material collected by eleven- to fourteen-year-old primary school students during 1937-8, and is separated in volumes by school, parish, townland and county, so that specific areas may be explored. These were gathered from the files numbered 771 to 776. They are all retold by children and have all the innocence and enthusiasm of a child's imagination, combined with the aural tradition that was still very much alive at the time.

In 1937 a collaboration between the Department of Education and the Irish National Teachers Organisation resulted in this wonderful scheme being initiated to encourage schoolchildren to collect folklore and local history from their areas. Over a period of eighteen months, some 100,000 children in over 5,000 National Schools in 26 counties in the Republic of Ireland took part. They were asked to look at different areas, including folklore. It contains myths, legends, songs, poems, riddles, cures, games, crafts and a whole plethora of other traditions and disciplines.

Most of the work was gathered by the children from their parents and grandparents, other family members and older neighbours. It is a truly remarkable collection of magnificent original material and a real treasure trove for anyone interested in folklore and folk traditions.

A FAIRYTALE BY NANCY BONROY, ROBERTSTOWN NATIONAL SCHOOL, NAAS, AGED 12 YEARS

Years ago there lived in Littletown a man named Jack Brennan. He was very poor. One day he had no food to eat, and his wife said to him, 'Jack get up early in the morning and go off and sell that cow'. When morning came Jack got up about five o'clock and started for the fair. When he was passing by a place in Littletown called a Rath he heard music and dancing. He was opening the gate to go in when a voice cried out, 'Go back Jack Brennan,' and at the same moment the place became all dark and in front of Jack stood a little man with a red cap on him. He asked Jack how much did he want for the cow, and he said thirty pounds. The little man told him to put the cow into the house which he showed him. Jack put the cow in it and the little man told him to take as much gold and silver as he wanted. Jack filled his pockets with gold and silver and started for home. When he went home he told his wife and she said to put the gold and silver into a sack. He did so and went to bed. When they got up the next morning they got a great surprise. Instead of a sack of gold and silver there was sack of old withered leaves in it.

The Children of the Rath by Peter Daly, Blackwood, Robertstown, aged 13 years

Once upon a time there lived a farmer. He used to lose a big number of cattle every year. There was a rath on his land. One night a very small man had asked him if he lost many of his cattle. The farmer said he did. The little man told him to take the fire himself every night and to sweep the hearth clean. The farmer did as he was told and he lost no more cattle.

The next year he had a black cow that was after calving but gave him no milk so he decided to sell her. He brought her to the fair and sold her. That evening when returning home by the rath he saw sixteen children and they crying out, 'Where is our cow? What are we going to do for milk.' The farmer then decided to get back the cow at the loss of the milk. He went to the man that he sold her to and gave him back his money and got the cow. He left her by the rath where he saw the children. He did not milk her for three years and then she disappeared. He said nothing to anyone about her. Seven years passed when one morning he went out to the stable and what did he find but the black cow back in her own place in the stable and four lovely black cows and four lovely white calves along with her. That was his reward from the 'good people'.

The Devil and Doctor Foster by John Booney Kilmore, Enfield

Once upon a time there was a doctor in Summerhill named Doctor Foster. He was very fond of the playing cards. One night a man was sick and needed a doctor. The man lived about two miles outside Summerhill. At about nine o'clock at night an urgent call came to the door. The doctor did not go at once because he was too well engaged playing his cards. When he had finished his game, which was about half an hour later, he told the groom to saddle his horse. When the horse was at the door he mounted him and rode away.

When he went about a mile of the road there was a barren and for quickness sake he took it and went that way. He was grumbling about being out in the cold and wished he were at home again. He was then about halfway through the barren but then all of a sudden the horse shied and the doctor looking to see what was it saw. He saw two men sitting by a camp fire playing cards. They halted him and asked him to join them in a game. He dismounted and tied his horse to a tree and sat down to play. They were not long playing when the priest came along also on horseback. They asked him to play but the priest refused and said he was in a hurry. He asked the doctor to come with him but the doctor said he was time enough. The priest then went on his journey. After a while the doctor let a card fall. He stooped to pick it up and he saw the cloven foot and he knew it was the devil. He immediately rose to go home. He untied his horse and mounted him but the horse would not stir. He dismounted and beat the horse but he would not go. He left the horse there and walked home. As he left he looked back and saw that the devil was gone. He then went to the priest and apologised to him for not going with him.

The Good People by Maureen Lamberr, Robertstown NS, Naas
14 November 1935, aged 13 years

Years ago an old neighbour of ours had many farms in Grangehiggin, Kilmeague, Naas, County Kildare. On one

of the farms stood a rath. He considered it spoiled his field
and he wanted to till it. He had three workmen and he
told them he would dismiss them if they did not plough it.
They were very sad at the thought of being dismissed; but at
the same time were afraid to interfere with the homes of the
good people. They had to do as the old farmer told them,
for they had wives and children depending on their wages.
They started to plough the rath. When they came to the
middle of it the man who was following with the horses said,
'Good people don't blame me for cutting up your home'.
A little man dressed in red came up through the ground.
He had a very sorrowful face and he said, 'What do you mean
by putting me out of my home?' The man told him that the
farmer would dismiss him if he did not do it. The fairy told
him not to go on ploughing or he would be sorry. He gave
the fairy a promise he would not. When he went home in
the evening the farmer was ill in bed. The workmen told
him what happened and the old farmer dismissed him. In a
week's time the farmer died. Sometime after the farm was
sold and the man who bought it gave this poor man back his
job. But the rath never could be tilled.

THE THREE DOGS BY PAT DOWING
ALLENWOOD MIDDLE

Once upon a time there lived a king with his four sons.
His wife died and he married another woman. One day she
brought the three eldest princes into the forest and changed
them into three dogs. The three dogs' names were Anvilhead,
Hearwell and Runwell. Anvilhead could knock down stone
walls with his head. If he gave anything a puck he killed it.
Hearwell could hear anything, no matter how far off it was.

He could hear the grass growing. Runwell could catch any-thing in the world, no matter how swift it was. The youngest prince was too young to be changed into a dog and so the witch queen put him in prison. He grew up to be a fine prince. One day he managed to escape from the prison. The witch could change herself into a hare, or a fox, or a wolf, and when she saw the young prince escaping she changed herself into a hare and took her magic wand with her. The prince kept running until he came to the forest. The three dogs saw the prince and they waited for him. They knew who he was. They also know the witch when she was changed into a hare, or a fox, or a wolf. When the prince came to the dogs he asked them their names, they told him and after a while he fell asleep.

All this time the witch in the shape of a hare was coming to change the prince into a dog. 'Here she comes,' said Hearwell. The very moment Runwell saw her he took after her. The witch ran very hard but Runwell caught her all the same. 'Hold her till I give her a puck,' said Anvilhead. Hearwell gave Runwell a hand to hold her. All of a sudden the witch changed herself into a fox and escaped before Anvilhead came up to kill her. The next day she came in the shape of a fox to the wood. Hearwell heard her coming and told Runwell. Runwell caught her and Hearwell gave Runwell a hand to hold her until Anvilhead would come up. They made up their minds not to let her escape this time but she turned herself into a wolf this time and fought them before Anvilhead came up. They were very disappointed at having let the witch escape twice. They thought that sooner or later their brother would be changed into a dog. After a while they agreed upon a plan. When she came the next time, the three of them would wait until she was about a yard or so away from them and then they would rush upon her and kill her. After a while Hearwell said he heard her coming. They waited for her. When the witch saw no one coming she thought her way was clear. She was coming in the shape of a wolf. When she came near to them they rushed upon her. Anvilhead gave her a puck but it did not kill her, so she changed herself into a hare. Runwell caught her and nearly killed her. When she was dying her two front paws changed into two hands. In her hand she held a wand. With it she changed the three dogs back into three princes. The four of them then went back to the old king.

BIDDY THE BESOM BY PAT DOWING
ALLENWOOD MIDDLE

Long ago an old woman went around with besoms, which were a type of broom … a bit like the ones you might think of a witch riding on. She gave them to the farmers' wives in exchange for bread and milk. She was called 'Biddy the Besom'. A beggarman went around here long ago and he was called 'Jack the Skinner.' Jack Kelly was his real name but he went around looking for old goats. He used to skin them and he sold the skin afterwards.

22

COONAN'S FIELD

This poem is based on true events. When I was a child growing up in Kildare I had to use my imagination a lot as there was not a whole lot do living in the countryside. But when a child's imagination is combined with a wild and wonderful countryside there is no telling what wonders will be created. We lived next door to an old house owned by the Coonan family. We were always told not to play in the big field next the house but as a child this made it all the more adventurous. I felt it was important to write this poem as when my young daughter asks me what it was like being a child all those years ago, I can always show her this poem.

When I was a kid
Do you know what I did
To avoid all things boring and tragic?
I would step inside my mind
And there I would find
A world full of adventure and magic.

I would play a fantastic game
And nothing would be the same.
A stick for a sword, I would yield
An old bin-lid was my shield
And off I go to fight monsters
In Coonan's Field.

A great oak tree was my castle;
I'd hop and swing from branch to bough
With a youthful ease that escapes me now.
I'd climb right up to the very top
And nothing in this world
Would make me stop.

Now Coonan's Field I'll have you know
Was no place for the faint-hearted to go
For in it you would find monsters big and small.
Each had its own battle call
But the one that I feared most of all
Was the ferocious emperor troll.

He had red bulging eyes,
A fierce pointed nose,
Sharpened teeth,
And serrated claws,
Not to mention
Those terrible snapping jaws.

Avoiding cow dung
And wandering cattle,
I would approach my foe
Poised and ready for battle.
Then I would roar with all my might,
'Come on Troll, let's have a fight!'

At last I would face him
With my sword and shield,
Two sworn enemies in Coonan's Field.
I'd roll, I'd jump, I'd dodge and duck,
Avoiding his killing blows
In the mud and the muck.

It was all going well,
Then I ran clean out of luck.
It didn't take long before
My wellie-boots got stuck.
He came at me, hurling boulders and rocks.
'Forget about this, I'll fight him in my socks!'

But then I heard a voice beckoning me;
It was my mother calling …
'It's getting late, come in for your tea!'
I stood and looked at my fiendish friend,
Wishing this night would never end
In this wonderful world of pretend.

Well that was a long-long time ago
And so much has changed
As we all know,
But when I feel sad a little bit low
I know there is still a place
In my memory where I can go.

And I think of that little boy
Conquering his own private Troy
With a stick for a sword
An old bin-lid for a shield,
Off fighting monsters
In Coonan's Field.